A. S. Hale.
1928

THE AMBASSADOR

·The MCo·

THE MACMILLAN COMPANY
NEW YORK · BOSTON · CHICAGO · DALLAS
ATLANTA · SAN FRANCISCO

MACMILLAN & CO., LIMITED
LONDON · BOMBAY · CALCUTTA
MELBOURNE

THE MACMILLAN CO. OF CANADA, LTD.
TORONTO

The Ambassador

THE LYMAN BEECHER LECTURES
ON PREACHING,
DELIVERED AT YALE UNIVERSITY
IN THE MONTH OF APRIL, 1928

"We are ambassadors for Christ"

BY THE

RT. REV. JAMES EDWARD FREEMAN
D.D., LL.D.
BISHOP OF WASHINGTON

New York
THE MACMILLAN COMPANY
1928

Set up and electrotyped.
Published, October, 1928.

PRINTED IN THE UNITED STATES OF AMERICA
BY STRATFORD PRESS, INC.

Dedicated to my faithful and highly esteemed friend, a Christian ambassador and Cathedral builder, the

HONORABLE HENRY WHITE.

Entered into life eternal, August 15th, 1927.

FOREWORD

THESE lectures lay no claim to originality. They are the results of observation and experience covering an active ministry of thirty-four years spent in three city parishes, i.e., Yonkers, Minneapolis and Washington.

In preparing these lectures I have felt that the preaching office must be considered as essentially related to the pastoral and priestly ministry. A ministry that is partial must prove ineffective, no matter how excelling its gifts may be in any single aspect of it. If the "field is the world," then as Ambassadors for Christ we must discover our relation to it, and apply ourselves assiduously to its large concerns. The present-day restlessness, which characterizes the life of the Church, demands that those who minister its sacred office shall rediscover those indispensable elements that constitute at once its largest effectiveness and security. The need of a closer study and evaluation of the ministry and its place in our modern life is conspicuously evident.

With humility and the consciousness of the limitations which both observation and experience afford, I have undertaken this task. The one motive that has dominated my thought has been to endeavor to see this great office in its fullness, to see it as transmitted to us from the hands of our divine Lord, to see it in its upward reach after attainment. The empowered man is ever the "man sent from God." With a firm belief in the continuing and ever-broadening influence of such a ministry I submit these lectures to my brethren, praying that what I have written may serve to give freshened interest and quickened zeal to those who are laboring for the increase of his Kingdom.

I acknowledge with grateful appreciation the valuable assistance given by my chaplain, the Rev. Raymond L. Wolven, in preparing the manuscript for publication, and in reading and correcting proof.

Bishop's House,
Washington, D. C.,
Eastertide, 1928.

CONTENTS

FROM THE ORDINATION SERVICE

And now again we exhort you, in the name of Jesus Christ our Lord, that ye have in remembrance, into how high a dignity, and to how weighty an Office and Charge ye are called: that is to say, to be Messengers, Watchmen and stewards of the Lord; to teach and to premonish, to feed and provide for the Lord's family; to seek for Christ's sheep that are dispersed abroad, and for His children who are in the midst of this naughty world, that they may be saved through Christ for ever.

Have always therefore printed in your remembrance how great a treasure is committed to your charge. For they are the sheep of Christ, which he bought with His death, and for whom He shed His blood. The Church and congregation, whom you must serve, is His Spouse and His Body. And if it shall happen that the same Church, or any member thereof, do take any hurt or hindrance by reason of your negligence, ye know the greatness of the fault, and also the horrible punishment that will ensue. Wherefore consider with yourselves the end of the Ministry towards the children of God, towards the Spouse and Body of Christ; and see that ye never cease your labour, your care, and diligence, until ye have done all that lieth in you, according to your bounden duty, to bring all such as are or shall be committed to your charge, unto that agreement in the faith and knowledge of God, and to that ripeness and perfectness of age in Christ, that there be no place left among you, either for error in religion or for viciousness in life.

Refer to page number five hundred and sixteen (516) of the Book of Common Prayer.

THE AMBASSADOR

THE AMBASSADOR

CHAPTER I

HIS CREDENTIALS

This lectureship was founded for the avowed purpose of giving greater efficiency and distinction to the high office of the Christian ministry. Upon the platform created for its exponents have stood men of excelling gifts. For over half a century, one by one these great exemplars of the prophetic office have sought to emphasize anew both the privileges and the opportunities of the minister of Christ. This period of time has wrought mighty and far-reaching changes in this ancient office. It would be safe to say that no single period in the history of the Christian Church has placed a greater strain or a severer test upon the ministry than the one covered by this lectureship. What lies ahead no living prophet may venture to forecast. If the past fifty years have been fraught with perplexities and difficulties and perils, it is safe to say that the immediate future gives no promise that the way of our pilgrimage is to be one of easy accomplishment or freedom from conflict. It has been well said that "the cause which can be won to-day is not worth fighting for."

Let us admit at the outset that a church without

problems is not to be desired, and a ministry that avoids rough ways and refuses hardships, contributes to enervation and issues in loss of power. The whole record of the Church's life is one that speaks of progress through trial. Overcoming difficulties, rising above seeming defeats, contending with adversaries, yes, even facing crucifixion, its mighty heralds have enriched the chronicle of human experience with deeds of heroism that find no parallel in recorded history.

As a matter of fact, its most luminous periods have been those of its greatest struggles. This we dare not forget in an age made soft by indulgence and enervated by luxury. To call men to the ministry with the assurance that it provides ease and freedom from harassing problems, is to divest them of those chivalrous and heroic elements that in other times have given the office its greatest distinction and power.

No age that has gone before exceeds this one in the demands laid upon the minister of Jesus Christ, and no period has presented larger opportunities and privileges to the ambassador of Christ than the one in which we now live. It is to the man who seeks to be an ambassador we address ourselves; the ambassador who regards his office as the highest and holiest given to men; yes, the ambassador who holds his authority as from the hands of Christ and his field of service as coterminous with human life the world over.

Thus we approach this lectureship in the sure confidence that what it stands for and represents, has a larger and more vital significance to-day than at any other time since it was founded. If the problems it presents are more difficult, if the hour is one that is weighted with complex and conflicting issues, we address ourselves to the tasks in hand with the deepened conviction that, what we are commissioned to, as ambassadors for Christ, is of greater moment now than ever before. Let us dare to believe with Carlyle that "a new splendor of God" must presently emerge "from the heart of this industrial age," and that the sovereignty of Christ is the momentous issue of this eventful hour.

The very fact that our generation is passing through one of those recurring transitions, wherein far-reaching changes in thought and practice are being effected, makes the theme that engages our attention one of compelling interest. The estimate you and I place upon our office as ministers of Christ's Church must have a determining effect, not only upon our own course of action, but upon the future of the Church itself. That there have been within recent years, disclosures of inefficiency in the Church, must give any thoughtful man pause.

The mere fact that there are places in which the Church is showing, under the most favorable circumstances, growth and increasing usefulness, is no evidence that the situation at large is normal and satisfactory. Every now and again we meet men who occupy places of peculiar advantage in the ministry who, by reason of their own luxurious and prosperous environment, refuse to see any danger or confusion in the present situation. They deliberately shut themselves off from the facts in the case and refuse to be interested in anything that suggests peril or impending disaster. That their little or big exclusive garden patch is well tended and prospering, is their selfish and sole concern. Again, there are others whose pride of sect or denomination is such that they are unwilling to consider any condition that lies outside their own exclusive coterie or fellowship. These belong to that insular and provincial class, all too numerous among us, who, like the Pharisee of old, would thank God that they are not as other men are. There is a third and a still more reprehensible group that, in their search for self-ease and comfort, would say with Louis of France: "After me, the deluge."

We are assuming at the very outset that all these symptoms of insular thinking and practice are local and not general. We may, we believe, assume that, taken by and large, a wholesome concern is felt to-day for the Christian institutions of the world, and an increasing desire is manifest to so stabilize and strengthen them, that they shall render their largest service to an age that is seeking for new light on darkened pathways. As indicative of the spirit of those whose apprehensions render them unresponsive to the present need, let me quote from a letter, not long since received from a highly conscientious but greatly bewildered man, whose concern for the Church has, for the while at least, paralyzed his hopes and accentuated his fears. Asked to give to the erection of a Christian institution that is designed to render a great, national service, he wrote: "I am afraid that Protestant religion is on the decline, and it will take something more than Gothic churches to revive it."

With his conclusion concerning the insufficiency of

multiplied Gothic churches we find ourselves in perfect agreement; to his declaration concerning the decline of Protestantism, we can only say, if the statement is measurably true, now is the time to buckle on our armor, to lengthen our cords and strengthen our stakes for the most aggressive crusade that the world has ever known. If we are willing to allow, and there are signs that confirm it, that the Church has lost ground during recent years, then in the spirit of that thin red line that in a crisis fought a winning battle with its back to the wall, let us at any and all costs undertake an adventure for Christ and His Church that shall, please God, issue in a widespread and freshened revival of the Christian religion. We will not declare a truce with the enemy, we refuse to accept any terms that seek to impair the influence and power of an institution that we hold to be fundamental to the highest and holiest interests of mankind. There is serious need for statesmanship and the employment of the best strategy in the present situation. There may be need for a new alignment of the forces and possibly for a change in the personnel of our leaders. That there is need of consolidating the ranks and a simultaneous and aggressive forward movement is conspicuously evident. Beyond the acknowledgment of these palpable facts we refuse to go. "Our importunity is God's opportunity," possibly never more so than now, and if something of the spirit that characterized the early Church can once again seize us, we may dare to believe that we shall presently see the greatest advance the Church has made in its entire history.

We do not conceive that in these lectures we should come to you to propose palliatives for long-standing ills; but certainly we must in all fairness and frankness face conditions that are real and not fancied, and with boldness expose their weaknesses and seek to correct their faults.

We were told but a few years ago that unpreparedness menaced the security of the nation, and even now we are being admonished in days of peace that there is a kind of supine indifference that issues in more dire consequences than war itself. Every institution to-day is seriously considering its possible weakness as well as its potential strength. New and more scientific calculations and plans are being made, and security and efficiency are receiving larger consideration. Let us not, in any fancied assurance as to our impregnability, regard ourselves as immune to the ills that attack old as well as modern agencies and institutions.

God has given us a mighty task, we have been working at it with measurable success for nearly twenty centuries. We have witnessed such changes in human conditions under its influence that they would seem to suggest that a miraculous power had been working in the hearts and minds of men. We have witnessed the increasing power of Christ in his world and we have seen one stronghold after another yield to his invincible sway. History and experience alike, have demonstrated the utter fitness of His plan to redeem men and to give them a fuller, richer and more abundant life. Of these things we are reasonably assured and confident.

Therefore, we are not apologists for an effete and

outworn system that has proved inadequate to meet the needs of men. It may at times have suffered at our hands, we may have signally failed to do our part in bearing testimony as to its potency, but it survives in spite of our bungling practices and misdirected zeal. The miracle of it all, is its persistence; it outlives all the faults and follies of its exponents. It still maintains its place and holds the affection of men the world over.

We disavow all interest in those who, approaching life to-day, see only that which is shadowy, and are filled with fear as they behold the seeming break-up of an existing social order upon which is builded our boasted Christian civilization. God knows, we have again and again proven unfaithful to our great trust. We have been guilty of substituting the commandments of men for the doctrines of God. We have employed means and agencies that were wholly out of consonance with His divine will. Arrogance and self-pride have obscured His designs and purposes. Notwithstanding all this, His church still stands as the greatest single agency for lifting human burdens and cleansing human hearts mankind has ever known. As a regenerative force there is nothing that remotely compares with it. Divided as are the forces, futile as are many of our endeavors, to this divinely ordained institution men's hearts and minds still turn, with high hopes and joyous expectations.

Describing the prevailing power of this divine Master, a modern dramatist makes the centurion who stood at the cross say, as he addresses the lonely and sorrowing Mary:

> I tell you woman, that this dead son of yours, disfigured, shamed, spat upon, has built this day a kingdom that can never die. The living glory of him rules it. The earth is His and He made it. He and His brothers have been molding and making it through the long ages; they are the only ones who ever did possess it; not the proud, not the idle, not the vaunting empires of the world. Something has happened on this hill to-day to shake all the kingdoms of blood and fear to dust.

Let us dare to believe that he spoke with prophetic insight; let us dare to believe that the "vaunting empires of the world" are presently to feel the sway of His scepter. Better that we stand for this, cost what it may, than that we stand forever in the shadows of an unending Gethsemane. You and I hold that Jesus Christ is the supremest need of the present hour, that without Him, civilization with all its accumulated treasures is jeopardized and imperiled.

We believe that His teachings, unobscured and undiluted by our conceits of learning, are indispensable to world order and peace. In our better hours we dare to oppose and resist the forces that would displace Him. Latterly we have been so busy in our laboratories, studying microscopically some new theory of doctrine, some elusive and obscure shade of meaning in our textbook that somehow we have lost that moral and spiritual robustness that arrests and holds the unfailing attention and interest of men. While we may satisfy our own curiosity and regard ourselves as those to whom some large revelation is vouchsafed, we contribute little to advance His kingdom, or to lend strength and courage to sinning and despondent men.

Our ambassadorhood can prove of no avail in such critical days as these, unless with chastened humility it yields utter obedience to Him who declared: "I am come to seek and to save that which was lost." We have largely substituted systems and forms and organization for deep-seated, life-controlling religious convictions. We have purveyed to our people a "comfortable gospel," that has in it nothing that demands heroic self-discipline and self-surrender.

Says a brilliant English preacher as he surveys the present situation:

> Unless the Church is a means towards the sanctifying of common life, unless our worship here is a means to make every place and every time a time with God in his presence, unless our prayers and our sacraments help to hallow the whole of the rest of our lives, unless our Eucharist helps us to see every common meal as a sacrament, unless the consecration of our churches helps us to consecrate every house and dwelling and shop and street, then we had better not have a church at all; for we are falling into the grievous error of making certain things sacred at the cost of making everything else profane.

Startling words these, but not too startling to one who really senses the seriousness of the present situation.

Only as we evaluate the facts in the case, only as we come to realize the responsibility and opportunity that are ours, shall we rise to the full stature of an office, that still holds its place of peculiar distinction and power in the estimation of thoughtful men and women. Other professions have to do with some special sphere of human endeavor, ours has to do with the whole compass of life. Other callings have their authority and sanction in some agency or institution designed to meet some special needs of society; ours has its authority and sanction in the word of Him who said: "All power is given unto me, in heaven and in earth."

Thus, we come to affirm the priority and indispensableness of our ministry. Thus, we plead a cause that transcends all others. From a cross the Savior looked out upon an age as morally decadent as any known in human history. He saw the remnants of systems that had tragically failed and broken down. He was the victim of their cruel and wicked designs, and yet with sublime confidence he saw the ultimate triumph of His cause and the universal spread of His kingdom.

The conditions that confront us to-day will hardly compare with those that met His vision. Terribly tragic as have been these recent years with their sad story of human pain and struggle, titanic as have been the forces that have wrecked thrones and shaken to their footings the entrenched and long-approved systems of government, the world to which we minister to-day is more receptive to the heroic gospel of Christ than it has ever been before. The very calamities and tragedies of life have made imperative the message we are commissioned to give. The urgency of the present situation lays upon us responsibilities and affords us opportunities, such as no preceding age has accorded the ministry. To believe less than this, is to fail to see the advantage which the present situation affords. That it calls for and demands men of sterling worth and unusual gifts is clearly obvious. It was said of the small tribe of an ancient people that it was composed of "men who had understanding of the times, to know what Israel ought to do, and all their brethren were at their command." Our age calls persistently for this type; men who have the genius to rightly evaluate conditions, who can penetrate beneath the surface of things, and understanding the needs, minister to them.

The late President Wilson in his last message to the world declared: "Our civilization cannot survive materially unless it be redeemed spiritually. It can be saved only by becoming permeated with the spirit of Christ and being made free and happy by the practices which spring out of that spirit." With clear vision he saw the perils that threaten to engulf our existing order, and that the only hope of preserving the best in our domestic, social and economic life resides in a new emphasis upon the supreme values of things spiritual. With like outlook President Coolidge but recently declared: "All our learning and science, our culture and our art will be of little value, unless supported by high character. A trained intelligence can do much, but there is no substitute for morality, character and religious convictions. Unless these abide, American citizenship will be found unequal to its task. The strength of a nation is the strength of its religious convictions."

That these men of large vision have sensed and rightly appraised the situation, is a further indication of the obligation that is ours. What they hold is but the expression of a growing and world-wide conviction. The most striking aspect of the present outlook of men, the world over, is their belief that Jesus Christ has given the one remedy for the ills that disturb and harass us.

George Bernard Shaw will hardly be charged with undue leaning to the pronouncements of the Christian Church, and yet in his latest year he has avowed his unfailing belief in the indispensableness of the Christian religion. "This I know," says he, looking at life at seventy, "men without religion are moral cowards. The cause of Europe's miseries was its lack of religion." Thus, the voices of men to-day are emphasizing both the criticalness and the urgency of the situation.

Are we sufficiently alive to the high claims of our mission? Are we prepared to face a world that is crying out for spiritual leadership? Can we by any fair, consistent and reasonable means so consolidate our forces, that they shall have at least the semblance of unity? These are questions that constitute a great challenge to the man of God, and no half-hearted response will serve in the present situation. With this brief word as to the world's need of what we have to give, let us reverently apply ourselves to a more careful consideration of the office and work of the Christian ministry.

HIS CREDENTIALS

"We are ambassadors for Christ," declared the great apostle. What the ambassador is, to and for his country, implies first of all, the imposition of authority. He is what he is by reason of his credentials; he is vested with a power that, conferred upon him by his government, guarantees to him a place of recognition and distinction. He has a prescribed and definite duty, and the success of his mission is conditioned, on the one hand by his sense of authority, and on the other, by his unfailing fidelity and utter devotion to the cause to which he is committed. As a minister plenipotentiary he has his assignment, his prescribed sphere of influence, and the success of his administration will be determined by his fitness, his loyalty, his equipment, his technique, and the recognition of his perils. His rewards will come to him only as he demonstrates his capacity to recognize the indispensableness of these things. He will come to his place of power and usefulness only as he wholly consecrates himself to the high office to which he is called.

We cannot think of the ambassador of a government holding lightly his great commission. We cannot think of him as being dilatory or careless in the discharge of his duties. His is a weighty and highly responsible task, and upon his fidelity and devotion, the prosperity, security and peace of his constituents largely depend.

The office of the Christian minister, rightly conceived and exercised, carries with it powers and responsibilities not less worthy and important. However men may have failed to live up to its large privileges and opportunities; however unworthy they may have been of their sovereign's confidence, it still stands in the estimation of men, as the highest and holiest of occupations.

Those who have most vitally and efficiently exemplified it, have been those who at all times and under all conditions recognized the divine source of their gifts and powers. The outstanding characteristic of the Christian ministry, as well as its most distinguishing mark, is ever and always its high sense of mission. Its chief and most compelling virtue is found in its representative capacity. It stands for a definite purpose. "The profession which consists in being something," said Mr. Woodrow Wilson, "is the ministry of our Lord and Savior, and it does not consist of anything else." It accepts its authority from a divine Master and says to the world in terms of assurance: "That He should be made manifest, therefore am I come." It is not so much the representative of a system as of a personality.

As it has its commission from Him, even so must it ever recognize its responsibility to Him. In the inception of this office we read that the Master commissioned men, giving to them definite instructions, a definite task and a definite assurance of His unfailing and continuing presence. He sent them forth to an unfriendly world, He admonished them as to the difficulties and perils that awaited them; He promised them stern hardships, suffering and possible martyrdom, but with the assurance of ultimate success and triumph.

It was no soft or easy task that He gave them, but one that called for the most heroic qualities. Never before in the history of mankind had such an obligation been laid upon the minds and hearts of men. Never before had such a field of service been presented, nor such large powers conferred.

The utter selflessness and devotion of those early disciples have been the admiration and wonder of all the generations following. Their flaming zeal, their consciousness of power, their chivalry and heroism, and their amazing conquests, constitute a story of achievement of incomparable worth.

Through succeeding ages the ambassadors of the cross, in spite of persecution, have carried His message to a world that was coldly indifferent to its appeal. They have risen to their greatest heights of power where opposition was strongest; they have languished almost to extinction where their efforts had the applause and favor of men. Poverty has not hindered them, increasing riches have frequently checked their advance and chilled their enthusiasm. It is literally true that "when the Church had wooden chalices, it had a golden priesthood, when it had golden chalices it had a wooden priesthood."

In unbroken ranks, down through the centuries these empowered men have persisted; the story of their accomplishment finds no parallel in the annals of human history. If we seek to disclose the secret of their extraordinary daring and endurance, we shall inevitably find it in the conviction they held concerning their Christ-given authority. They believed that to them were committed by their divine Lord, the large concerns of His kingdom. Where this sense of authority has been most evident the Church has witnessed its greatest advance, where it has been indifferently held, the Church has seen its most serious decline. It is conspicuously evident that there can be no effective leadership without it.

It would be of little worth that we proceed to discuss further the theme assigned us, unless we are prepared to recognize this fundamental fact concerning the Christian ministry. We believe that this ministry is as indispensable to a well-ordered, happy world to-day as it has ever been; hence, we approach that which this lectureship calls for, with the freshened conviction that the subject we have in hand is of vital moment, and never more so, than in this pregnant and eventful hour.

We do not have to defend the importance and validity of an office that bears upon the deepest and dearest concerns of life. That "man is incurably religious" and that the demands of his soul can be met, only as we exercise those gifts committed to us, we confidently affirm. There are those who question or disesteem the value and importance of this divinely ordained office, but there is nothing new or unique in their contention. Over against their bold assertions we have ample proofs as to its supreme value and usefulness.

We are not met to carry on a controversy, we are met to maintain the supreme place and power which the ministry has occupied in all the concerns of human life. That there is need of fresh emphasis and larger insistence upon its divinely imposed authority, we believe is urgently demanded.

We do not wish to begin these reflections upon the ministry with undue conceits concerning the exalted place this office holds. We are minded to heed the word of its supreme exemplar, where he said: "He that is greatest among you shall be the servant of all." Too often have pride and arrogance cost the Church humiliation and defeat. Too often has a self-confident and autocratic ministry reduced it to the low plane of mediocrity, and brought upon it the just condemnation of honest men. A kind of conceit of orders ill becomes a ministry designed to present to the world the life and teachings of the humble Christ. Nothing that we shall say here, seeks to unduly magnify that which we believe discloses its greatest excellence when adorned with humility. Priestcraft is a dangerous and repellent form of excess of assumed authority, wholly out of consonance with the will of Him whose credentials we carry. "He made himself of no reputation," was recorded of our great exemplar. Officiousness or fussiness are too often assumed to be expressions of authority. Insistence upon certain prerogatives or rights on the part of him who is called to minister to a people, has again and again produced a situation that effected lamentable results. We have known men of marked ability whose ministry signally failed, because of this tendency to undue self-exaltation.

The sources of authority upon which our social and economic order is based, find their genesis in certain customs or practices that have grown out of long and exacting experience. Trade and barter, the conventions of polite society, represent as we know them to-day, the results of continued experiment and practice. From the cave man with his rude habits to the modern member of society, we trace the gradual rise of the customs that to-day are accepted as indispensable to well-regulated social intercourse. Our complicated economic system is no accident; it has come to us as the result of laborious and painstaking study and effort. It is by no means perfect, but it is indispensable for all that.

What of the Church and its orders? Shall we regard them as the result of chance, as the inevitable consequences of a man's demand for the expression of his religious instincts? Is there no authentic, well-conceived body of evidence as to their origin, their gradual growth and expansion? Shall we believe that here it is only a question of adaptation of means to meet the capricious whims and fancies of an ever-changing world of men and women? Is there no authority for what we hold of faith and practice? No well-ordered and well-adapted methods that spring out of Christ's teachings and those of the early Church that still constitute the major claims of this institution of which we are the leaders and exponents? Shall we regard the vital things of our faith, along with its sacraments as ordained by Christ, as matters that we are at liberty to receive and practice with reverent obedience and devotion, or disregard them as our wills or convenience may dictate? Is there no word of finality, no enduring and indispensable authority that has been handed down to us as the later exponents of a system, divinely conceived? Is the Church a group of individuals whose mental conceits must determine what is fit or unfit, what is practical or impractical, to meet the spiritual yearnings and aspirations of men and women? Then, obviously, we may readily abandon all that has gone before, dismiss as unworthy of our consideration all that history and tradition have disclosed as of value, repudiate or disregard the customs and usages of a so-called "Apostolic Church," and abandon orders, systems and sacraments that have approved themselves by long usage and practice to the moral and spiritual enrichment of the generations that are past.

A modern church by this standard of judgment cannot have anything in common with what has gone before. It needs neither creeds nor systems, it must be utterly flexible and adaptable, it must accommodate itself to every changing fashion and adjust its habits, practices and teachings to the new and fanciful conceits of those to whom it essays to minister. Thus, a modern up-to-date minister, with individualism carried to the nth degree, would reform the world and effect a new heaven and a new earth wherein dwelleth righteousness.

Have we any striking evidences as to the efficiency of such a course? Does variety here, an excess of emphasis upon individual tastes, submit such irrefutable and unchallengeable proofs, as to make its case sound, substantial and convincing? How many churches built upon such a strikingly original and utterly novel theory have survived? We would not disparage in the Church's leaders originality or independence of action, provided they recognize always their relation to order and system; but where they regard themselves as independent of the institution that conferred upon them their office, that commissioned them to service; where they set individual opinion above constituted authority, we cannot but regard them as doing violence to that which alone justifies a valid and consistent ministry.

I am quite aware that I am accentuating here the value and authority of organization, exalting system and order as indispensable to an efficient ministry. Even so, we may find abundant evidence for our argument in every form of organized life with which we have to do. Our political, social and industrial systems, have their being and their continuing efficiency in laws, regulations, conventions and methods; and their beneficent service is afforded those who are unfailingly obedient to them. Where that much heralded and misinterpreted term, "self-expression," becomes so utterly selfish and individualistic that it runs counter to all rules and regulations, it becomes a form of anarchy, destructive of the large interests of a well-ordered and well-conceived society.

We shall surely reach a tragic state when we are all so committed to an extreme form of self-expression that we have ceased to understand or practice self-repression. A day when every man indulges in personal liberty to such an extent that he does that which is right in his own eyes, independent of what its effect may be upon others, will mark the beginnings of disorder, and the break-up of those things that, by long experience, have proven indispensable to the orderly ways of decent and profitable living. That the Church through its ministry should become so loose in its practices, so vague and indefinite in its teachings, so flabby and colorless in its vain effort after popular favor, that it ceases to stand for anything of enduring moral and spiritual worth, with no sense of a background of authority, means that it is nearing the day of its dissolution and abandonment.

If your ministry and mine is simply that which we individually conceive it to be, if it is a profession that rests its appeal upon some formula prescribed by a little coterie of men, who in their quest for something modern and original would part company with historic systems and ideals of faith and practice, then let us reckon with the consequences that inevitably follow such a course of action.

"What is the constitution between friends?" was the facetious observation of one who regarded an orderly state and orderly procedure as works of supererogation. There is much of this light and flippant talk to-day and it invades every precinct of our life. Let it not invade the precincts of the Church. Jesus definitely commissioned men, He definitely gave them instructions as to their office and its functions; they went forth empowered as ambassadors of their Sovereign, and their conquest constitutes a record of great distinction and high accomplishment. Of them it was said: "They that have turned the world upside down, are come hither also." They approached with confidence fields that seemed sterile and unresponding; they invaded territory that was coldly and repellently indifferent; they endured every form of ignominy and shame; yes, they boasted of their sufferings and went gladly to martyrdom for their faith. For more than three centuries they persevered in the face of persecutions, and thousands of them gave their lives for the mighty cause they represented. Increasingly their sense of authority grew, and ultimately the eagles of Rome capitulated to the despised cross of the Nazarene and wrung from the lips of an apostate and cruel emperor the declaration: "O pale Nazarene, thou hast conquered."

Every study and observation of this early crusade, yes, every study of the crusades that have followed, has made evident the power of men who believed they were invested with an authority from Him, that brooked no interference and acknowledged no defeat. That this sense of authority must be restored, this dignity of ambassadorhood maintained, is conspicuously evident to-day. We cannot go on, except to inevitable defeat without it.

Says a distinguished writer in a recent essay:

> The claim of the Church to authority, rests upon two principles; the social nature of man and the lordship of Christ. As Christians we are disciples, pupils, learners, and our loyalty is to our teacher; and we are also Churchmen, members of a fellowship, inheritors of a kingdom, and our allegiance is to the great community whose life we share. Through the Church we become "heirs of all the ages," and enter into the whole religious experience of the race.

That the Christian ministry of our day has lost something of this sense of background, this investment of authority is clearly evident. That it must be recovered and reëstablished is also evident. Only recently we saw a letter written by a physician to a clergyman in which frank avowal was made of apostasy from the Church, and serious misgivings expressed as to its usefulness and validity, and yet in conclusion the writer affirmed that what made him still hopeful of recovering his faith was the evident conviction and deep sense of authority the preacher disclosed in his message. "You have made me feel," he concluded, "in spite of my doubts that, the only institution that stands between us and a return to savagery, is the Christian Church."

It is this kind of sense of authority we have in mind. Not that of some rude, vaunting, blatant dogmatist, who cries his wares like some huckster, condemning those who cannot and will not accept his narrow and ignorant interpretation of God's will and purpose concerning men; no, not this kind have we in mind. Rather that of another whose speech is not vehement with condemnation, but winsome with the persuasion of Him who "spake as never man spake."

Our whole ministry is conditioned by this sense of authority, the consciousness of "a power not of ourselves," a power given us to exercise our office as ambassadors of the most High. In majestic phrase Isaiah felt and expressed it when he "saw the Lord sitting upon a throne, high and lifted up and His train filled the temple." "Whom shall I send?" was the searching inquiry. "Here am I, send me," was the swift response, and from the holy presence he went forth clothed with power.

We recall a thrilling passage in Valleri's life of Savonarola. The dying Lorenzo the Magnificent had sent to San Marco for the despised monk to absolve him. Wearily and anxiously he waited. At length

Savonarola appears. Standing beside the dying man he demands renunciation of evil deeds and full repentance. Lorenzo is disposed to yield, but upon one point he is adamant, he will not yield. Again the monk enforces his claim. Full repentance and restitution, else no absolution. Lorenzo refuses and turns his pale face to the wall. There is a moment of tense, dramatic silence, then Savonarola gathers his robe about him, and leaves the room. The mighty prince could not cajole or bend him. He dies unshriven. There is something in the bearing of the man of God that commands our admiration and reverence.

This of which we speak is the conspicuous and tragic lack of our age. It discloses itself in the pulpit, in the intimacy of the pastoral relation, in conference room and assembly. We do not deny that God utters Himself to other than those to whom, in a peculiar sense, He commits His oracles; we do hold that to whom this sacred ministry is given, the sense of this revelation must be evident.

"Take thou authority," is the language of the ancient ordinal; it is a tremendous charge, weighted with responsibilities of indescribable significance, and suggestive of opportunities infinite and varied. The test of the value if not the validity of our orders, may be largely determined by what they actually convey to us of the sense of a transmitted and hence authorized ministry. It is ever and always, the "man sent from God," who compels a reverent and responsive hearing. We cannot believe that God acts in the large concerns of His kingdom without design or plan. We cannot believe that our divine Master commissioned men to act as His representatives to the world, without investing them with definiteness of authority.

In that solemn hour of His withdrawal He supplemented all that had gone before with a final word of direction, assuring them of His presence always, even unto the end of the world. With this assurance they went forth to an unresponsive and ungenerous world and wrought a miracle in resisting all opposition and overcoming all obstacles. Every reformation that has followed has had this kind of leadership.

It is the supreme need of this wistful age to-day. Men are groping for truth, they are yearning for a new manifestation of spiritual power; they are insisting that speculation and negation shall give place to deep conviction, born of experience. They will heed only Him whose message and whose ministry bear the unmistakable evidences of a divine imprimatur. Dr. McComb is right when he declares: "Never have men longed for faith as they long for it to-day. They call themselves agnostics, skeptics, non-religious, but at heart they yearn for a vision of spiritual order; and the man to whom this revealing vision has come will find an audience in the wilderness." The supreme desire of St. Francis was, that in his body might be disclosed the stigmata, the very branding marks of his oneness with Christ.

We can hardly convey through anything we may say here, all that we feel concerning this sense of mission. It is best exemplified in those who have been the beacon lights of the world in their several generations. The world is clamorously calling, calling as it never has before, for a ministry whose validity is disclosed in the life and teachings of him who has companioned with Jesus and learned of Him.

In his notable description of the battle of Waterloo, Hugo concludes his stirring page with these words: "Was it possible that Napoleon should win this battle? I answer, No. Because of Wellington? No. Because of Blucher? No—Because of God! Waterloo is not a battle, it is a change in the front of the universe."

Brethren, we are witnessing again a vast change in the front of the universe. Shall the new world see its victories won through the growing skill and genius of men? Shall it be through human conceits, ungoverned and unregulated by the recognition of a divine plan? Shall we not boldly and with sure confidence answer, No. God, the Eternal, must be made regnant in the hearts of men. To such a high and holy and empowered service He beckons us on.

> A mightier church shall come, whose covenant word
> Shall be the deeds of love. Not CREDO then—
> AMO shall be the password through the gates.
> Man shall not ask his brother any more,
> "Believest thou?" but, "Lovest thou?" and all,
> And all shall answer at God's altar, "Lord, I love."
> For Hope may anchor, Faith may steer, but Love,
> Great Love alone, is captain of the soul.

CHAPTER II

HIS FITNESS

I have already suggested to you the need of a fresh appraisal of the office and work of the Christian ministry. I ventured to remind you that fundamental and indispensable to its efficient service is its sense of mission, its consciousness of authority. I need hardly remind you that in other callings and professions this is also true, but not to the same degree as in this holy office. I warned you that the sense of mission does not disclose itself in arrogance or the assumption of autocratic habits of speech and action. Humility, that excelling virtue, is less conspicuous in our generation than it once was. I recall that our Lord repeatedly emphasized the need of it in His intercourse with His disciples and that His own ministry gave it freshened emphasis.

That He gave to His followers and through them to those who were to come after them, an authority such as had never before been transmitted to men, is one of the most self-evident facts of the Gospel narrative. He sent forth that body of peasant disciples to be His witnesses, the empowered exponents of His resurrected life. Of them we read that "with great power gave the apostles witness of the resurrection." It was to a group of men who had failed Him in the crisis that this power was given. Pentecost came to these men bringing with it an increase of this strange power and as Lecky, the critical student of the intellectual and moral development of Europe maintains, invested them with such extraordinary gifts that they effected results beyond anything the world had ever before witnessed. Edward Gibbon bears like testimony, in his monumental work on the Roman Empire. I dwell for an instant upon all this, because I am clear in my conviction that our present age is asking each one of us concerning his ministry: "By what authority doest thou these things?" I would certainly hesitate to press upon my generation the claims of my office, or to urge its indispensableness, did I not believe that it is of divine ordering, and that it holds its authority from the pierced hands of its supreme Master. The late Dr. William R. Huntington once observed to me that "the seemingly lost note of our modern pulpit, is the dogmatic, the note of certitude," and that to this more than to any other single cause he traced the impotence of the modern pulpit. I would have you give deep consideration to this for it is primary and fundamental. This morning I want to endeavor to discuss certain elements of fitness that need emphasis, because they bear vitally and immediately upon the situation that confronts us.

If authority, the sense of mission, is indispensable, then we may venture to affirm that fitness, with all that it implies, calls for our most serious consideration. I am addressing a body of men who have assumed or will presently assume the weighty obligations of a great office. I share with them these obligations and over a ministry covering four and thirty years I have been increasingly conscious of the value of these things to which we address ourselves this morning. While by temperament and training we may hold different views as to methods of administration, in essential particulars we are all compelled to recognize certain norms or standards that inhere in our common service.

What I shall say to you to-day, may seem homely and commonplace, but it has an intimate relation to an efficient and compensating ministry.

There are many themes and many subjects that command our interest to-day. The swift and alluring current of life, its rich and varied hues and colors, its unparalleled development along many lines, its mechanical contrivances and inventions that bewilder us more than the vivid imaginings of Jules Verne, all this is both fascinating and diverting. In spite of it, yes, because of it, those of us who assemble here must regard the theme which this lectureship calls for as of transcendent importance, possibly never more so than now. It would be of little worth that we come here attempting to submit to you some conceits or theories we may hold concerning the ministry. The value, large or small, that may accrue to what we shall say must depend wholly upon the accuracy of our diagnosis of present world conditions and the relation we, as ministers of Christ, may bear to them.

We disavow at the outset any sense of infallibility. We can only give you out of an interesting and varied experience, our own mature and deliberate convictions as to the place, worth, and privilege of this high office. We can tell you what we have found profitable and helpful and what, with charity toward all and malice toward none, we have found hurtful and unprofitable.

No matter what else a man may carry in the way of equipment, grace of person, or gift of tongue, the indispensable thing is that somehow, someway, he shall convey to his constituents the idea that he carries credentials as an ambassador, the minister plenipotentiary of God. Nothing do men sense more than this. To use Joubert's fine phrase:

> You may do what you like, mankind will believe no one but God; he only can persuade mankind who believes that God has spoken to him. No one can give faith unless he has faith; the persuaded persuade, as the indulgent disarm.

To even approach such a theme as the one assigned us, without the deep conviction that the Christian ministry is the highest and holiest of all occupations in which men engage and that it demands first of all and above everything else, the sense of ambassadorhood, would prove fatal to all that follows. You remember John Brierly's bold affirmation? "Let our prophet come with a new mandate for the soul upon his lips and though his speech be in the dialect of a Galilean peasant, the people will hear him gladly." There is a mysterious and undefinable quality that inheres in the man who possesses in a large degree the God-consciousness. He may lack many gifts and graces that are called for in other professions; he may, like Lincoln, be homely of face and ungainly of bearing; he may have little that would give him place or distinction in pulpit, rostrum or drawing-room, but once we come into his presence and listen to his message we feel the force of his personality, the indescribable spell of his genius and the irresistible power of his utterance. Said Canon Newbolt: "Men will yield to goodness where they will not yield to argument."

I think it was Thackeray who observed that: "The Lord writes a letter of credit on some men's faces which is honored wherever presented." Jowett and Brooks are striking examples of what we have in mind. In this very lectureship Brooks maintained that preaching is sixty per cent personality. That "religion cannot get on without an incarnation" is axiomatic; this implies a personality that reincarnates and reproduces Him of whom it speaks.

That a certain kind of special training, a measure of refinement and culture if you will, coupled with the gift of utterance, are the sole requisites of the ministry, is a fallacy that has resulted in many sad disappointments and failures. I once commended to the late Bishop Potter for the ministry, a young man who I believed possessed certain unusual gifts of mind. The wise Bishop responded by reminding me that while all that I said was doubtless true, he would further remind me that other gifts than those I had named were indispensable; did the young man in question possess them? I was compelled to admit he did not.

More and more as we have noted the rise and fall of certain so-called "promising candidates for Holy Orders," we have become fixed in the conviction that this is a profession to which it is dangerous to invite a man, unless the man himself feels a profound sense of fitness for its high claims. In another day men were "called" to this sacred office, latterly we have adopted the draft method, and not to the profit or enrichment of the Church. Possibly this more than all else accounts for so much of eccentricity in the pulpit, and the employment of unseasoned, and sometimes grotesque methods in an effort to cover up conspicuous defects and deficiences.

In Dr. Storrs' *Preaching Without Notes,* he portrays a situation in a seminary of his day that, let us believe, is not widely known now. He describes a class of three men with whom a professor of theology was vainly struggling; they were a curious mixture of various and utterly diverse types. Says Dr. Storrs, "One was a skeptic, another a dyspeptic, and the third a Swedenborgian." He adds with a touch of grim humor, the Professor resigned and entered the alluring field of politics; but no comment is added as to the disposition of the students.

Time was, in England, when a household divided itself into the "fit" and the "unfit," and all too frequently the latter were assigned to the ministry, while the more robust entered callings that demanded the sterner qualities of an aggressive and vigorous manhood. The army prescribes certain tests to be applied to those who seek admission to the service. These tests are applied with impartiality to all who come. We would have better conditions prevailing to-day, if like care were exercised with those seeking Holy Orders. "Endure hardness, as a good soldier of Jesus Christ," was the apostolic dictum. Such an injunction repels the anæmic and the unfit, and while it may make the numbers few, it does make them reasonably select. Why this holy office should be given without discrimination to those who are unfitted for the more robust tasks of life, we cannot comprehend. Surely there is no profession, no task to which men aspire, that calls for more of sturdy manhood than this one.

I am altogether cognizant of the fact that Frederick Robertson of Brighton was so impaired physically that the army rejected him, while the Church readily took him. On the other hand, his is a case where physical deficiencies were counterbalanced by an amazing mental alertness, coupled with a profound sense of mission. True, he died at thirty-seven, broken in body, but be it remembered he left to his Church a legacy of spiritual achievement such as it has rarely witnessed. What we are attempting to stress more than all else, is what we call the sense of fitness. This we maintain is utterly fundamental and all else is conditioned by it.

I am quite aware that in some men this is a matter of growth and development, even so, let it be, but be it must, or we only add further to the impaired risks of an institution that is already heavily embarrassed.

The call to the heroic in the ministry is little heard in our day. We have quite forgotten that "the blood of the martyrs is the seed of the Church." We hear little of those who would say with Paul: "I am crucified with Christ," or "I will rather glory in mine infirmities," or, again, "My strength is made perfect in weakness." Little wonder is it that such a man disturbed the lustful pastimes of Nero's household, or that his ministry was known and reflected in the royal palace.

This spirit must be recovered if the Church is to resist and triumph over the titanic forces that to-day are arrayed against it. Say what we will, it is this quality of utter self-giving, of complete consecration or willingness to go to martyrdom, if need be, for Him whose credentials we bear, that is the supreme demand of this critical hour. "From whence does the Church draw its continuing power?" asks one of the modern critical annalists of history. "It is from the crucified Son of God upon the cross," is his answer.

Reproduction of this spirit is what our flabby age calls for. Men will resist argument, they dare not contend against a life that will give its all for Christ. "With well doing," says the Apostle, "ye may put to silence the ignorance of foolish men." If "all men are commanded by the saint," then it is largely because the saints who have wooed the world have been of the heroic sort.

The "Manliness of Jesus," as Thomas Hughes interprets it to us, is most appealing. He presents to us a Master whose habit of life was strongly masculine. Wherever and whenever such an interpretation is given, it compels reverence and emulation. "The disciple is not above his Lord," and the exhibition of a consistent, and under all circumstances, strongly masculine interpretation of Jesus, is one of the most persuasive forces we know. Such an interpretation is costly, and it ought to be. If a soldier will give his all for flag and country, we who follow in His train cannot afford to give less.

Our profession more than all others is caricatured and derided by the interpretation given it on stage and screen. It may be that all too often the picture is not ill drawn. The weak and the effeminate, the soft and the anæmic are, like the poor, always with us; and in the crises that repeatedly arise in our civic life the absence of the leadership of the man in orders, tragically witnesses to another lost opportunity.

I know of no profession that lays a larger claim upon the heroic element than does the Christian ministry. I know no place where fearlessness is more urgently demanded than in this ancient office. There are causes all about us that challenge the best that we have to give. There are opportunities for taking leadership that, while demanding personal inconvenience and sacrifice, are nevertheless, fascinating and appealing. A metropolitan bishop of rare gifts stirred the imagination of a great city and aroused it from its supineness when he dared to challenge an intrenched and corrupt political machine, and by his course he drove it from power and won new adherents to the Master whose example and practice he emulated.

The youth, particularly, are drawn to this type of spiritual leadership. They will answer to the call of the heroic, they are unmoved and unresponsive to that which is weak, colorless and insipid.

The "call to the colors" challenged the finest we had in college, shop, and workroom. It was a call that implied self-surrender, possiby making the supreme sacrifice, but it was readily answered by millions. It was a great adventure. Something approximating it must once again lay its claim upon the heart and mind of the men of our generation. A religious appeal that has in it nothing of the demand for sacrifice, or the surrender of self to the high claims of the heroic Christ, gathers few adherents to His standard.

The greatest asset the Church has to-day, is to be found in its missionary leaders, who, "counting not their lives dear unto themselves" have gone forth to difficult, sometimes sterile fields, to bring the illuminating and emancipating gospel to those who sit in darkness and in the shadow of death. What Hannington did in the Uganda or our own Bishop Rowe has been and is doing in Alaska, constitutes a stirring and inspiring chapter in the modern prosaic annals of Christian service. Young "Borden of Yale" may have lacked a large knowledge of what higher criticism has done to clarify the text of Holy Writ, but the nobility of his life and the utter consecration of it to an ideal of Christian service, thrills us with admiration and quickens our dull and torpid imagination.

Strike out from the record of Christian endeavor the story of these heroes of the cross, and it is shorn of its most fascinating and appealing element. Those chaplains overseas that wielded the largest influence, though unarmed, dared all to prove their love and devotion. Donald Hankey tells us that while much of the faith of the British Tommy was inarticulate, nevertheless he understood the meaning of the heroic life of Christ and felt His presence; the presence as of the "White Comrade."

One sometimes wonders whether we do not need in our ministry, the "moral equivalent of war," to give it stability and staying power. To think of it in terms of ease or the gratification of some intellectual pursuit, an office that gives large range and liberty to one who would, untrammeled, walk the "cool, sequestered vales" of life, is to stultify it and render its great cause unproductive. Some one speaks of "that majestic indolence so dear to native man"; avoid it as you would some devastating plague.

May I be pardoned for alluding to a charge given me by one of my own distinguished preceptors, namely, the late Bishop Henry C. Potter, toward the close of my theological course. Said he, "You have hitherto been employed as an accountant in a great corporation, you have been compelled to follow daily a definite rule of life. Your time was not your own, neither must it be in the future. Set for yourself a definite norm or standard of service, have fixed habits of study and for doing parochial work; do not be a machine but be orderly, only so will you come to approximate any degree of excellence in the office of a minister of Christ."

The value of such an injunction must be clearly evident. Carelessness or slovenliness, or worst of all, indolence here can have but one issue, namely failure. Other men to whom we minister are compelled to observe definite rules in the big game of industry and commerce, so must we; else we shall lose caste, and our preaching, however eloquent, fail of its high purpose.

I know full well, other and better men in this lectureship have said all this and more, but I venture to enforce it afresh, because this age of ours is growing more and more critical of our office, and a very proper demand is being made upon it to give substantial evidence of its worth-whileness and value. "I came not to be ministered unto, but to minister," "I am among you as he that serveth," these were Christ's definitions of His conception of His own ministry.

I shall surely be consistent if I venture a further observation that certainly needs mentioning here. I refer particularly to the recognition of what we commonly call the amenities or courtesies of life. It may seem an inconsequential matter to incorporate in a lecture of this kind, but I am bound to believe that we are judged, more largely than we think, by what we are and do in these seemingly small matters of ordinary daily intercourse with men.

In so commonplace a matter as correspondence, the prompt and courteous acknowledgment of letters, our profession is singularly recreant. I have heard a distinguished presbyter of the Church boast that he did not concern himself with such trivial and unimportant matters as letters. On the other hand, Phillips Brooks was famous for the meticulous care he took with his correspondence. An unanswered or ignored note is an insult to the one who indited it. Failure to promptly acknowledge the receipt of a gift, however small, to some cause in which we are enlisted, embarrasses the giver and renders unworthy the recipient.

It would not be difficult to cite cases, where failure has attended a ministry otherwise gifted, the immediate cause of which was carelessness in matters of this kind. Again, we recall other pastorates, crowned with success of the best sort, undistinguished for unusual preaching gifts, but unfailing in acts of courtesy. "Be ye courteous," might well be the conspicuous legend in all our studies. Of all places in the world, a boor in this high office is an anomaly and an offense.

It has been suggested, not without much merit, that every candidate for Holy Orders should be required to spend at least three years in some commercial pursuit, in order to form orderly and fixed habits of life. It has been further suggested that in view of this, a dispensation from Hebrew and Greek might be in order. I am confident the latter suggestion would meet with the hearty approval of the undergraduates. A new chair in our colleges and particularly in our seminaries, designed to instruct men in habits of refinement and to promote gentility, would prove a boon to the ministry and a source of infinite satisfaction to the laity.

After all's said and done, piety, plus gentility, constitute the major adornments of this important office. Said a large prospective giver to a clerical solicitor: "I was not so much interested in the object of your appeal as I was in the manner of your presentation of it. Here is my check." It can be demonstrated that it actually pays to be a gentleman under any and all conditions.

A further observation that is pertinent here, has to do with the matter of meticulous care in the handling of Church or so-called "discretionary funds." I recall the case of a young clergyman who had a fine stone church built for him by the wife of a man to whom he was in the habit of sending, periodically, detailed financial reports. His fine consistency and business sense so influenced her that, though unknown to him, she gladly provided a handsome gift that gave him his first start upon a notable career.

Carelessness in financial matters is a conspicuous weakness of the clerical profession. It does not require a course in accounting to be accurate in such things, it does require a sense of responsibility and a conscience void of offense. Seemingly inconsequential as these observations may be, I can assure those who are contemplating a ministry of real value and efficiency that they are indispensable to the making of a fit man for this high and holy office. Cleverness, mental alertness, a genius for preaching, skill in parochial administration, all these must have as a background, yes, as a foundation, these sometimes disesteemed, lesser gifts and practices.

A further and by no means impertinent observation has to do with the clergyman's habit of life in the world of action. The day of the "sporting parson" may be gone, but the day of the indiscreet is still with us. No standard we set for Sunday may be lowered on Monday. No habit or practice we commend in our preaching may we violate in our own daily contacts with men.

Consistency of living is an invaluable and indispensable aid to an efficient ministry. Worldliness, a habit that would

> Condone the sins we have a mind to,
> By damning those we're not inclined to,

is reprehensible and disastrous. That we *do* have standards, that we will not yield, nor permit our households to yield, to the changing loose conventions of society, is imperatively demanded of us. A single indulgence in some worldly pursuit frequently works havoc to an otherwise distinguished service.

He who thinks such a course commends him to men, is reckoning without knowledge of their minds. Those to whom we preach, who for themselves demand liberty in all things, even to the point of gross indulgence, demand of us, and rightly so, that we shall remember at all times the dignity and sacredness of the office we carry.

There is a kind of effort after popular favor, a disposition to appear broad and tolerant, that is fraught with the gravest consequences to our calling. I do not mean in any sense that we are to be prigs, or censorious and ungenerous critics. I do most certainly mean that under any and all conditions we are to be clearly distinguishable from those who know no standards and refuse to recognize the rules of common decency. "Avoid all appearance of evil," is a safe maxim.

These things must be reckoned with by him who would essay the rôle of a minister of Christ. The tragedies of unformed and broken careers in this holy office, illustrate in a most solemn and striking way, the folly of indulgence in those things that are wholly alien to our calling. We must dare to be different, dare to be conspicuously different, if need be, that we shall not bring reproach and shame upon the cause to which we are committed. To wear always the "white flower of a blameless life," may mean at times humiliation and embarrassment, nevertheless so must it be.

To stand alone for principle is far better than to lose one's identity in the crowd, the crowd that knows neither principle nor honor. In an age in which the "repeal of reticence" is so conspicuous, no man who believes in things that are pure and honest and of good report can afford to be indulgent or careless.

I have put these things that make for fitness thus early in this course of lectures, because I am confident I am giving expression to what is increasingly and properly demanded of the clergy in this critical age. Homely, these observations, you say; obvious, you suggest, yes; so homely and obvious that sometimes they seem to be largely forgotten or ignored.

I have said nothing thus far about physical fitness, all that obviously, is presupposed. Physical fitness or physical health is stated by Huxley to be the first requisite to success. The habits of the ministerial profession are not as conducive to physical robustness as are those of other occupations and professions. Possibly here again this is due to the fact that we set for ourselves no definite norm or standard of daily practice. It is certainly evident that lethargy of the body produces lethargy of the mind. Too frequently we find it easier to spend an afternoon in a comfortable chair with a pipe and a book, than out in the open in pastoral visiting, or in some form of healthful recreation. Any form of indolence tends to mental inertia. If our bodies are the temples of the spirit, then they demand unfailing care. Habits of study we must have; periods for mental and physical refreshment are indispensable. They are as important to the maintenance of fitness, pulpit fitness, administrative fitness, as the mental gymnastics in which we indulge.

I recall that the late Dr. Weir Mitchell once told me, that he had repeatedly admonished his friend, Phillips Brooks, concerning the need of keeping his body strong and well for the large tasks he exacted of his mind. "God has given you a superb physical frame," he repeatedly told him, "and unless you care for it, some day when you least expect it, you'll find it breaking beneath the strain."

His admonition proved accurate, but too late heeded, for the great master of assemblies did break at the early age of fifty-seven. A comparatively slight malady found his system a prey to its ravages. Our office is an exacting one, calling for mental poise and alertness; these can be maintained and insured only by persistent care and rigid self-discipline. To keep his body under control, to make it a perfect machine, obedient to his will, compels one to recognize always the utter value of self-denial. An anæmic physical condition is bound to issue in an anæmic mental condition. We cannot and we dare not go to our pulpit, or indeed to our parochial duties, unfitted by a day or a week of careless living, or weakened through practices of self-indulgence. Arnold Bennett's little book, *Twenty-four Hours a Day*, has much of value for the man who would live and work efficiently. It insists upon plan and system, it demands the recognition of the first principles of healthful living. I heard a close observer of preachers once say concerning his pastor that he had "good visibility." He was implying that, quite apart from the substance of his message, he made a good impression when he stood before his people. The man who lacks this has a handicap to overcome before he has uttered a word.

Our seminaries would do well to make physical fitness a primary requisite for those applying for orders. They would do still more for the good of the Church if, in their curriculum, they insisted upon some form of imposed physical discipline, which a candidate for the ministry was required to take. To be "thoroughly furnished unto all good works" means a sound mind in a sound body. Someone has said that "the Church's future, the whole question of its teaching, services and organization, will be conditioned by its relation to life's physical basis."

It is true that there have been men, and women too, who, in their effort after holiness, have laid upon their bodies such stern discipline that they came at length to appear attentuated and ethereal. They have, these separated ones, with their rigorous fastings and ascetic life, given to the Church as an institution, certain gifts and qualities that we gladly and gratefully recognize and acknowledge. That they had their conceptions of holiness and that they came at length to approximate a high degree of sainthood, and like John on Patmos were given revelations, is certainly true. The Church has canonized such and given them place among its great ones.

Perhaps every age needs men and women of this sort, mystics, who believe that only as the physical is subjected to the hardest and severest discipline, can the spiritual be brought to articulate itself. Let us reverently pay tribute to these earnest souls and give them place in the hierarchy of the saints. You and I may be unworthy of such exaltation, but we are concerned here about a different and a more exacting sphere of service that calls for and demands a type of physical development that can meet the strain which a twentieth-century church lays upon its clergy.

I am by no means undervaluing the habits of the more cloistered life of the man of God, I shall deal more fully with that in another chapter. What I am here seeking to urge, is that kind of physical robustness, or if you will, that stalwartness of life, that constitutes the essential foundation of long-continued mental effort.

All of us may consistently strive for sainthood, for holiness, but let us remember that holiness means also wholeness. A starved and undeveloped body is a poor domicile for an energetic heroic soul. One is sometimes compelled to wonder, as he observes some of the examples of our profession, whether a "lean and hungry look" is the essential concomitant of piety. We cannot believe that it is. "He bore his great commission in his look," was the fine testimony concerning one who was the embodiment of his office.

When you find that you have lost facility, grown stale in the study, flee to the open, ventilate a brain that has grown dull; do to your mind what you do to your razor when it has lost its keenness, strop it with bodily exercise. If any habit in which you indulge has made you physically and mentally anæmic or lethargic, quit it. A torpid liver is responsible for many a dull discourse. A distinguished secretary of state said to me, "Most of my clerks come to the office in automobiles, I am one of the few in my department who walk. I cannot do a good day's work unless I get a modicum of exercise."

Paul pursued his trade as a tent maker, resisted a malady that hindered him, and literally rose on stepping stones of his dead self to higher things. John Wesley lived into the eighties and preached from three to five sermons a day, but he could not have done it, unless he had lived in the open. Outdoor life and preaching in his case, as in that of George Whitefield, had much to do with physical and mental vigor.

What a fine passage that is, "How beautiful upon the mountain are the feet of them that publish glad tidings." It is redolent of the fragrant and health-giving atmosphere of the great open spaces; it is suggestive of that buoyancy and exhilaration that proceed from long-sustained contact with the things of nature.

When Henry Ward Beecher had attained supreme heights as a preacher, he was wont to say he found his greatest mental recreation, as well as his spiritual exhilaration, in long periods of meditation and reflection by wood and stream, out in God's great world. As a matter of fact, and in speaking of it I surely do not commend it, his special periods for the actual forming and fashioning of his sermons were the few hours on Sunday morning, immediately preceding the service. This, however, was the mechanical part of his effort, the final work of arranging and planning; the real background, genesis and genius of his message was his close and intimate contact with and study of God's revelation of himself in men and things; in glowing nature, with its sermons in stones and good in everything. His workroom was the world in which he lived.

I am confident that we would have more persuasive preaching if we had more men of robust bodies. All that I am saying will compel you to consider certain habits of indulgence that need not be named here, but they are, as we individually know them in our consciences, habits that have a determining and detrimental effect upon our ministry. We cannot habitually indulge in them and get the results we seek.

Let us be very clear about it, what we are speaks more loudly than what we say. There is an eloquence in the restraints we put upon ourselves that, oftentimes, is more persuasive and compelling than the messages we utter. "Be ye clean, ye that bear the vessels of the Lord." Clean in body, clean in mind, clean in act.

I know I am trespassing upon a delicate matter when I speak of that which some one says is next to Godliness, but it needs to be emphasized again and yet again. You and I are dealing in a very intimate way with those who are finely sensitive to what we are in our persons. Many a one to whom we minister, more particularly the sick, is affected for good or ill by what we are externally. It is not a costly thing to be meticulously punctilious about neatness, about those refinements of person that bespeak a clean and regulated life. There is a coarseness that discloses itself in broadcloth, even as there is a refinement and gentility that are not disguised by homespun. You and I may not be exemplars of the mould of form or the glass of fashion, but we may be for all that, paragons of neatness. An unkempt appearance or a habit of shabby gentility may render impotent our best intentions.

I make no plea for fashionable ministers, I do make an urgent plea for an apparel "costly as thy purse can buy," and above all else for the most precise care that we shall not offend, through indifference to the niceties of personal neatness. I have known even a great sacrament of the Church to suffer in its administration, as the result of the failure to observe this cardinal rule. Again I say: "Be ye clean, ye that bear the vessels of the Lord."

The great exemplar of our office, unapproachable as He is, is the Master of us all. We are careful to study his mighty teachings, must we not be as careful to study His ways of living? True, we will not approximate in any large way this perfect model, but at least we may dare to reproduce something of its transcendent excellencies. If we are to compel men to see in Him the supreme example of what life should be, then surely we must, as his teachers, seek to be like Him. Manliness, considerateness, tenderness, a perfect understanding of what was in man, an unfailing confidence in his undeveloped potentialities, how shall we express in our poor way, the excelling gifts and graces of this Savior, Christ?

He found fitness for His great task in a long and lonely wilderness vigil. He lived, from early youth to the day He must needs go up to Jerusalem for the supreme sacrifice, out in the free and open spaces. He kept vigil with the stars in His lonely bivouac on some hillside. He found His chief fellowship with peasants on the highway; with fishermen in their boats; with men and women of the countryside. His mightiest utterance was delivered from a wayside pulpit; His most vital messages, bearing upon life's deepest mysteries, were spoken to pilgrims and wayfarers. He showed a physical robustness and vigor that never wearied. He attacked alone and unaided the traffickers in sacred temple precincts. His habits of life, as we reverently observe them, conserved the physical while they nourished the spiritual. How He rejoiced in making the weak, strong; the cripple to leap and sing; the unfits and the misfits, to find themselves, in a world of stern competitions. He literally rejoiced in the wholeness of life and ever and always He sought to strengthen bodies while He redeemed souls.

Our task, dear brethren, is even as His. It is a glorious task, fit for the ambition of the noblest. Its appeal is to those who have a passion for the souls of men. It lays upon us claims that call for physical strength, mental vigor, spiritual insight, a life well balanced and poised to meet any situation and issue as it arises. "Who is sufficient for these things?" He alone who is ready, joyously ready, to consecrate all that he has and is, body, soul and mind, to the greatest cause, the most fascinating adventure that has ever challenged mankind. With what nobler words may we come to our great service, than those of the ancient sacramental office: "Here we offer and present unto Thee, O Lord, ourselves, our souls and bodies, to be a reasonable, holy, and living sacrifice unto Thee."

THE AMBASSADOR

God of the prophets! Bless the prophets' sons:
Elijah's mantle o'er Elisha cast;
Each age its solemn task may claim but once:
Make each one nobler, stronger than the last!

Anoint them kings! Aye, kingly kings, O Lord!
Anoint them with the Spirit of thy Son:
Theirs not a jeweled crown, a bloodstained sword;
Theirs, by sweet love, for Christ a kingdom won.

Make them apostles! Heralds of thy cross,
Forth may they go to tell all realms thy grace:
Inspired of thee, may they count all but loss,
And stand at last with joy before thy face.

O mighty age of prophet-kings, return!
O truth, O faith, enrich our urgent time!
Lord Jesus Christ, again with us sojourn:
A weary world awaits thy reign sublime!

CHAPTER III

HIS ASSIGNMENT

Every ambassador sent out by his government has his prescribed sphere of service. His portfolio which accredits him to a sovereign power, defines his office and fixes his limitations. He is clearly conscious of the high purpose and aim of his mission. On his own government's representations he is received and honored, not so much for what he is, as for what in his person, he represents. An ambassador is a man with power. Everything that has to do with his own country and that to which he is accredited is his chief concern. He occupies the place of an interpreter, a liaison officer. He fulfills his highest usefulness and efficiency when with dignity and unfailing fidelity he discharges his solemn and weighty responsibilities.

Our Mr. Page as ambassador to the Court of Saint James is a fine example of what we have in mind. By his splendid gifts of mind and heart he served his own nation and England in a great crisis. He was as much honored abroad as he was at home.

When the apostle speaks of himself as an ambassador, he expresses the conviction that he is primarily the representative of his sovereign. From him and him alone he has his commission and authority. His ambassadorhood is one that, in the language of Christ, empowers him to every nation and people. He is sent to all the world to preach the Gospel and to baptize men in the name of the Father and of the Son and of the Holy Ghost. He is an ambassador at large, and in the exercise of his office, he is to be no respecter of persons.

In the mind of every great prophet and evangelist this world-wide conception of duty has obtained. The most outstanding figures in this ancient office have ever been those who had the largest conception of both their privilege and opportunity. The kingdom of God is without boundaries or limitations. John Wesley insisted that the world was his parish—he was an ambassador-extraordinary and minister plenipotentiary to all men. The old Latin poet, Terence, said of himself and his field of operation: "I am a man, and nothing that is human is foreign to me."

It takes a truly big conception of what our ministry is, to render it effective. A great English statesman urged his countrymen to use large-scale maps to insure them against alarms, panics and general misunderstandings. Here is where little, provincial, parochial-minded men fail. They get a notion that they are set apart to a certain circumscribed field. They restrict themselves to some exclusive little coterie of congenial persons, and see nothing beyond the small patch of ground which they feel they are appointed to till. Their gardens may be very well and artistically developed but the fences they build only serve to mark their limitations and impair their wider usefulness.

Some one once observed that a man is as large as the community in which he lives. We do not believe it. Charles Kingsley lived and worked in Eversly, a rural parish of eight hundred souls, but he experienced no limitations and felt no restrictions. He lived and preached and worked for the world. Frederick Robertson never got beyond Brighton, but his glowing messages still live as incomparable examples of inspired eloquence. Our own Phillips Brooks occupied two notable pulpits in two great cities, but who will deny him a place among the makers and moulders of world thought?

We largely determine our field of occupation. We can be provincial and insular if we will, or we can become factors in shaping the habits and practices of our age and generation. Our ambassadorship is to the world in which we live, and while of necessity we must have our own special field for our particular attention, we can, if we will, regard our sphere of influence as coterminous with human life itself. That we grow intensively only as we grow extensively is unquestionably true.

This is where our higher sense of mission comes in—our belief in the unversality of the Church's enterprise. The pastor who zealously urges a world vision and a world responsibility upon his people, inevitably enriches his own immediate field. On the other hand, the pastor who thinks and works only for parochial interests, comes at length to find his work dull, stagnant and unproductive. We know of one theological seminary in this country whose chief aim it is to give its students the missionary impulse. It has sent more men into so-called "foreign fields," than any institution of its kind of which we have knowledge, and with what result? That it has an indescribable spiritual power and culture, an atmosphere if you will, that draws to it men of the most robust and vigorous type. Its glory is its real catholicity.

Some years ago, talking with one of the most spiritually-minded men of the Church, whose field of occupation was in a small community, I mistakenly observed to him that, for his rare powers and gifts his place of assignment seemed too small. Quickly and with fine enthusiasm he rebuked me: "My field," he said, "is what I choose to make it. This town comprises so many people, they are not all mine, but I consider myself responsible for the spiritual well-being of them all. I am not the pastor of a little group, I hold myself to be the pastor of the entire community." He was not seeking to proselyte nor was he narrow in his churchmanship, he was simply affirming the real extent of his field of operation.

If this spirit were more prevalent, it would disparage unwholesome rivalries and shameless competitions and would encourage that consistent rivalry that should exist among men who have a passion for souls. Doctor Melanchton Woolsey Stryker, a preacher of unusual gifts, once told me when he was President of Hamilton College that, while he had comparatively few students, he felt that his was a great privilege and opportunity, one that affected the country at large, in that he was helping to shape the characters of men who must be in their generation the makers of a nation's destiny. Elihu Root is one of those who from this institution went forth to be one of the greatest statesmen of his time.

You and I never know to whom we may be ministering, possibly some genius whose lamp may be lighted by the torch we bear—some youth in whose soul we are privileged to kindle a flame that by the grace of God shall never be put out.

There is a kind of parochialism that is deadly to both pastor and people. There is a kind of preaching that is so local in its outlook that it makes saints of the Simeon Stylites type. They may be good for local purposes and emulation but they are utterly valueless to the world at large. An expansive ministry may prove an expensive one, expensive in the exactions it lays upon us, exhausting in its demands, but it is the only compensating ministry in the long run.

It were well that just here we spoke of that catholicity of mind that looks not on the things of its own but on the things of others. We are much occupied these days in considering what may be done to fulfill the Master's dream of a united Church. Thoughtful men everywhere are giving heed to the condition we are in, by reason of our unhappy divisions. A united Church, we are told, may effect a happy and warless world. This, as a theory, we have tacitly accepted, but to what lengths are we prepared to go to effect it? Here again is where our insularity discloses itself. We are eloquent on occasion in urging unity, but to what extent do we promote it by our catholicity of view?

To the vision of men we present a condition that suggests "confusion worse confounded." Our programs for advancing Christ's kingdom at home and abroad are seemingly irreconcilable. We pray for peace, but there is no peace. We promote our individual work and till our fields as though a world's salvation depended upon our peculiar brand of churchmanship. The situation is tragic and the results lamentable.

We are all servants of a common Master and yet our ecclesiastical families have but formal intercourse and communicate only with certain reservations. This is in violation of the principle of coöperation and fellowship laid down by Christ.

That by temperament and conviction we are affiliated with and devoted to a certain form of religious expression, is both reasonable and consistent. This doubtless cannot be changed, nor need it be, nevertheless there are basic principles, fundamental truths to which we are all committed and hold in common. We believe that "there is one Lord, one faith, one baptism, one God and Father of us all." We may use different forms of words to express this concept. We may follow the ornate or the simpler forms of religious devotion and practice. Some may love color and symbol, some may prefer that which is somber and barren of ritual, these things will always be, in a world of men and women of varying types and dispositions. The vital question is, do they constitute barriers or cleavages that must forever separate and segregate us? Shall we ever reach that stage where we have so completely the mind of Christ that we shall know no competitions, saving those that kindle within us a greater passion for His universal reign in the hearts of men? We have gotten away, or at least we hope we have, from a day where the dimensions of ecclesiastical badges and the tints and hues of sacerdotal gaberdines challenged the finest scholarship of the academy.

In a recent meeting of some hundred or more army chaplains held in Washington we were profoundly impressed with the spirit of perfect comradeship and whole-hearted unanimity that characterized their discussions. True, they all wore one uniform but that was an external thing, their unity lay deeper than this. They were all assigned to different fields of service, they all ministered to enlisted men of every sort and kind, they all experienced like difficulties and problems. They all acknowledged that they held their commission from one Master. Did they all do their work according to some prescribed manual? Not at all; but the fact that they did not, did not affect their complete sense of comradeship. Their only endeavor was to discover who could best serve.

The same condition prevailed in Europe during the great war. It manifested itself everywhere. As a matter of fact, we might still be in the midst of this awful struggle had it not been for the consolidation, under their own national standards, of all the armies of the allies. Why in the name of God and for the sake of His Kingdom, can we not have that kind of an alliance, that form of agreement that shall make of us a League of Christian forces? We shall not love our own standards and ecclesiastical households less, but His Kingdom more.

I am speaking to men, young and old, who are His ambassadors; may I with deference and high regard say to them, your assignment is what you please to make it. You can be little or big, narrow or broad, insular or catholic in your point-of-view and practice, but make no mistake about it, your age is clamorously calling to you to reform your line and to consolidate your ranks. It is solemnly admonishing you that there is grave peril in the present situation. A crucified Son of God waits the consummation of his great prayer. Have we thc courage and the will to hasten its fulfillment? Brief and inadequate as this word may be, we should prove recreant to the obligation you have laid upon us, did we not utter it.

I belong to a Church that affirms an unbroken continuity from Apostolic days. I hold with devotion and deep affection to its ancient ways. I believe with all my soul in the consistency and beauty of its time-honored forms and usages. I would have it bring, with humility, its rich contribution to the whole family of Christian believers, and I would have it excel in zeal in promoting the extension of His kingdom among men. All this does not in any sense imply that I would have all men yield to my ways and habits of dress and form. There is such a thing as unity in diversity.

To a disciple who would rebuke one not of their company, the Master said, "forbid him not, for he that is not against us, is for us."

Let us not think that concordats carefully phrased, or "gentlemen's agreements" to hold the peace, or friendly gestures that are cold and formal, nor yet uniformity of practice, constitute unity. It lies far deeper than this. It is generous coöperation that grows out of understanding and mutual good will. It is a comprehensiveness and inclusiveness of love that does no ill to its neighbor; it is that kind of charity toward all and malice toward none that makes for peace and harmony; it is that loyalty to Christ that makes every man our brother who acknowledges his sovereignty and accepts his redeeming grace. We shall see a frictionless, non-competitive church when we come to make Him the sole object of our devotion.

To you who are going forth in the flush of youth, going forth to a world that refuses to understand the reasons for a divided Church, I commend this finer, nobler spirit of catholicity. "One is your Master, even Christ, and all ye are brethren." To realize in any large and satisfactory way your ambassadorhood, you must have singleness of purpose. A discursive Ministry, that attempts everything, is a fruitless, yes, and a futile Ministry.

You and I are not called to-day to be encyclopedists; nor are we given our commission to be meddlers in other men's business. We have our distinct place and it is sufficiently large to occupy all our thought and effort. When Lloyd George was asked what in his judgment were the supreme requisites for an efficient ministry, he replied, "There are in my estimate, four great essentials: he must be a good fellow; he must have a message; he must believe in it, and he must know how to deliver it. Where there is a man with a message and he can give life and fire to it, he can always fill his church." With most of his conclusions we find ourselves in agreement, especially the latter. What he may mean by being a "good fellow" we do not know, but, if he means that kind of flexibility of living that seeks for popularity more than for solid worth, we are hopelessly apart from him.

That our office calls for dignity and meticulous care in the matter of indulgences, we certainly hold. That it means a kind of detachment from the world we surely believe. Not the cultivation of a monastic habit on the one hand nor an air of superiority on the other. That Jesus differed from John, the forerunner, is evidenced in the Gospel narrative. He entered into the festivities of Cana, He found sympathetic fellowship in the home in Bethany; He went to be the guest of the despised publican, He proclaimed Himself the friend of the outcast and the forsaken.

That is a fine description that some one wrote of our office where he says, "The real craftsmen are the patient builders; the self-effacing, kindly, humorous, not painfully learned ministers, who in our country villages and crowded cities, pursue their task of bringing men to God and God to men. To them, if anybody, the man in the street will go when he wants help." He speaks truly of our office.

Only recently we met such a "man of the street" who was passing through a great mental crisis. He was in a "dry place, seeking rest." In his confusion he sought the comfort and solace of conference with a minister of Christ. He had come to the great divide, where life's deeper values were being made clear to him. He needed spiritual counsel. The story he related was tragically disappointing. "I went expecting an inspiration, some word of direction; of peace and assurance, I did not receive it. I asked for bread and I got a stone."

The man of God failed him in his crisis. No pulpit eloquence can compensate for such a neglected pastoral opportunity. Our ambassadorhood frequently rises to its sublimest heights in the intimate relation which is afforded with an individual life. Who can ever forget the incident of Brooks' visit to a poor washerwoman on a hot afternoon, or the fine humility he disclosed in ministering to her needs. No wonder such a man could preach.

Our sphere of influence is not some pulpit encircled with a brass rail, which we occupy twice a week, it is the larger world through which we move. Of Christ it was said, "He built no capital, organized no army, wrote no volume, but seemed content to strew His words on the vanishing winds," and yet these words spoken in obscure places have been carried to the outmost bounds of the world. If He had His sphere of influence, His assigned place with and among men, where do we find it? Surely in those closer intimacies that brought him into contact with individual souls.

Our whole system is builded on these fragmentary utterances. Indifference to the common pursuits of men in their places of daily occupation, issues in lack of sympathy, and lack of sympathy means loss of power. We are not appealing for a worldly church but for a churchly world; a kind of ministry that has fellowship with men and women in their unworshiping hours. To specifically define methods by which this touch of fellowship is to be effected is largely a matter for local conditions to determine. Here, as in preaching, rules and methods are often like patterns that have ceased to be fashionable.

Our primary place of power and influence is the home, and the loss of this essential relation to the family is the immediate cause of the declining pulpit power of our age. It is quite clear that the complexity of modern conditions of living has rendered more difficult this part of our work. It is also equally true that a disposition to over-organization, of which we shall speak later, has largely deflected the clergy from this vitally important office. The rector of a church in a metropolitan center, whose membership strength was the largest in his communion, told me that the whole genius and success of his work lay in an unbroken and maintained relation with every family and individual in his vast congregation. Another rector, now a Bishop, was so punctilious about preserving his pastoral relations with his people that he kept a record of the dates of important events, both happy and sad, in their lives, and from year to year on recurring anniversaries communicated with them by letter or telephone or a personal call. A laborious task, yes, but an altogether worth-while one, and one that gave him a place of power with his people that was the envy of his brethren.

As a former rector of large and important churches, I know full well that what I am urging lays a heavy toll upon the clergy, but if we are seeking to discover the real causes for a declining church membership and a loss of interest in the large concerns we represent, let us look for it where it is surely to be found. "What do you think of your minister?" was asked of an old Scotch woman. "What do I think of him?" she responded, "I would rather see him walk from the church door to the pulpit than to hear any other man preach." She had in him a personal friend, a spiritual guide, a pastor of souls.

The Protestant bodies have largely substituted machinery of the most costly and complicated kind for the old intimacies of parish life. It would be interesting to discover among those who have had long experience in the ministry, how well they know, by name at least, those to whom from Sunday to Sunday they preach. I am confident such an inquiry would prove embarrassing.

Our personalities if they are worth anything, are worth more than what we say, and the ministry of one personality to another has an indescribable value. "The key to the mass is the individual." One of the great churches maintains this intimacy of which we speak through its system of an enforced confessional. It has proved to be of the utmost value, especially in dealing with congregations of great size. It may have features that are unappealing, but on the other hand it has continued in force, with striking efficiency, through centuries of practice. At least it proves a point of personal contact and doubtless of large profit to those who follow its use.

What have we that serves as a substitute? Will an occasional reception with its formal handshake, establish a relation remotely comparable to it? The answer is immediate, no. Of all deadly, valueless, formal things, the average parish reception is the worst. It magnifies differences and emphasizes social distinctions and cleavages.

If we will not have an established confessional, let

us at least make easy and possible something approximating an intimacy, an intimacy on things spiritual, with our people. Our first and foremost assignment is to the individual, our diplomacy and skill must first be disclosed in our consideration for and treatment of individual souls. I am commending nothing less than this, else I shall be untrue to the great Exemplar of our profession from whom we have our commission.

The ambassador of a government does not deal with a nation, save as he does it through its chosen representatives. We do not press the analogy too far, for there is an accepted form of diplomacy that works secretly and in dark places, "Open covenants, openly arrived at," is a more worthy method. Victor Hugo once said that "every man has his own Patmos," his place of larger revelation. To be identified in some way with our people when they pass through this experience, better still to be the means of leading them to it, is our highest and holiest privilege. That is a noble conception of the ministry wherein the poet says concerning one who was faithful to his trust:

> . . . Men felt
> That in their midst a son of man there dwelt,
> Like and unlike them, and their friend through all.

There is a term used in the medical profession that finds application to our office on its pastoral side. "Preventive medicine," implies so safeguarding human life against the ills that assail it, that it shall be largely immune to them. It anticipates physical maladies and so orders and disposes life and its environment, that conditions that produce disease shall not find a fruitful field for their genesis and development. A preventive ministry is an effort to so regulate the habits and practices of life, through intimate knowledge and close contact with it, that the evils that undermine and destroy it shall find no field in which to germinate and propagate.

This kind of preventive work is effected only through personal knowledge of tendencies and personal attention to them. It cannot be done through the formal message, nor through impersonal organizations; it requires an accurate knowledge of those local conditions in which diseases of the soul find their most fertile and favorable centers of operation.

Our first work as ministers is that of diagnosis. Diagnosis goes before treatment. Remedial work is based upon accurate knowledge of the conditions it is designed to treat. All this comes within the sphere of our pastoral ministry.

To so identify ourselves with the lives of men and women that we shall know their susceptibilities, their tendencies, their weaknesses, gives us not only an accurate and sympathetic knowledge, but equips us to deal with them specifically and scientifically. The old family physician that we used to know as a personal friend and intimate of our household, may have lacked that kind of special knowledge that to-day has rendered treatment more scientific; but nevertheless, such a personality, familiar with every aspect and phase of our household, made of our family doctor the most respected and efficient person with whom we had to do. He was the confidant of all as well as the personal friend of all. We went to him with as much readiness as we did to father or mother.

I know that what I am suggesting in the way of a pastoral relation as the primary assignment of a minister, is largely out of fashion to-day, and that it is the most taxing form of service in which we may engage; I also recall that in this lectureship repeated emphasis has been laid upon it, but my contention is that we are now confronted with a situation more critical than has been known in our generation, and it is our business to discover why it exists, the causes that have led up to it and the means of correcting it.

That the home constitutes the laboratory of the pulpit is demonstrably true; that the pulpit is largely shorn of its power without that which the home reveals, is equally true. He is the greatest physician of the soul who knows the most about it. All our reading and studying, indispensable as these may be, must prove futile without this finer, more accurate, more sympathetic knowledge of which we speak.

Our assignment means more than parochial visitation and administration, it means identification with the most vital interests of the community in which we are placed. All common and so-called secular concerns must be sacred to the minister of Christ. Said the sturdy Apostle of old: "God hath taught me that I should not call any man common or unclean."

Very frequently we find men in this office showing a marked disposition to cultivate only those who temperamentally, socially or financially are congenial to them. They have a class-consciousness, and beyond a select few they find themselves out of their element,

Such men have no place in the ministry, they should follow callings in which such things are recognized and permitted. Of all anomalous things the snob in the ministry is the most impossible and reprehensible. This is a form of phariseeism that dishonors the office and brings it into disrepute. We doubtless must have our intimates, those who constitute the inner circle of our friendship; this is natural and consistent, but let us guard ourselves against making this circle so conspicuous that it comes to be a menace to our larger efficiency.

Our world of action is larger than that of other callings, it is more inclusive. To us everything and every one that comes within our sphere of service, is in some way our responsibility and our care. We dare not recognize too rigidly, classifications, and above all else, we dare not segregate men and women to whom we minister into those that are common and those that are refined. The worst we may say of a church is, that it is composed of the "fashionable" or "the rich." Little wonder is it that too often, especially in our cities, the poor, the laborer and the artisan find no place within the confines of God's house.

May I recall what Phillips Brooks said to the woman who was cleaning the floors of Trinity Church when she told him of her daughter's approaching marriage. She yearned to have the service in Trinity Church, but believed it impossible. "Such a place," she said, "is not for the likes of me." Swift came the answer of the great prophet and lover of men: "Yes, Mary, it is for the likes of you and the likes of me and the likes of everybody," and the girl was married in Trinity and by the rector himself. No wonder the people heard such a preacher and heard him gladly. If our churches to-day have lost sympathetic touch with great masses of the people, it is our business to reform our habits and to essay the rôle of Him, who ministered to peasant and prince without partiality and with a burning love for all. Big churches for the favored, humble missions for the poor; rectors and pastors for the rich, curates and assistants for the needy, are utterly unworthy practices, and too widely recognized to-day. May God deliver us from this blight of the ministry that is imperiling its widest usefulness and service.

No problem that confronts the church to-day, is comparable to that which has to do with its relation to the artisan and laboring classes. For one reason or another they are not in sympathetic touch with the church. Rightly or wrongly they regard it as an institution that is quite alien to them. This is more true of our own country than of the church in Europe and England. Our utterances on industrial and economic questions are discounted and it is not to be wondered at when our knowledge of these questions is limited and partial. Granted that the discussion of such questions does not come within the purview of our pulpit ministry, nevertheless there is possible a more sympathetic and understanding fellowship with those who respond readily and gladly to our personal touch.

May we testify from personal experience, to the value of a discriminating endeavor to bring the ministry of the church into closer touch with those problems that to-day constitute the chief barriers between our ministry and those who, in countless numbers, are beyond our reach. We have observed the wider recognition of the social implications of the Gospel, we have seen the church embark upon a new venture, known as "social service." We have seen, in our time, a freshened interest in those questions that have to do with equity and fair play in the common dealings of life. All this is certainly to the good and a distinct gain. That blunders have been made, biased and unintelligent opinions registered, dogmatic utterances without an adequate background of accurate knowledge given, is conspicuously true. Nevertheless the drift is in the right direction. The work done by the present Bishop of London in keeping touch with the masses of the people in that great city, and by other faithful ministers who have broken away from the old restrictions of parochial life, is worthy of study and emulation.

We are not pleading for a ministry that is meddlesome and recklessly impulsive, we do plead for one that recognizes the largeness and inclusiveness of its task as defined by the Master whom we serve. That our assignment has to do with these matters, that we are to bring the healing touch of the Gospel to those open sores that afflict mankind; in fine, that we are to be the guardians and protectors of those who most need us, is imperatively demanded of us. I warn you to exercise large discrimination and tempered judgment here, to be just and fair, both in word and in act. There is a happy mean between a cold conservatism and an untempered radicalism.

In the new age that lies before us, the church will suffer severe and just criticism if it maintains an unsympathetic and unresponsive attitude toward questions and issues that vitally affect the life of vast numbers of the people. It is difficult to set a norm or standard for our action, but opportunities will repeatedly present themselves where we shall be compelled to speak and act with frankness and decision, and speak and act we must, else we shall further jeopardize a condition that is already gravely imperiled. Let us be admonished at all times, as we survey the field of our assignment, that no vestments are so clean that they may not be brought into touch with market-place and work-room, no orders too holy for holy men of all orders.

One reason why much of our pulpit work fails, is because it lacks familiarity with the hard problems and difficulties of life. The great prophets who have stirred men's souls, filling them with high resolves, have ever been those who were themselves aflame with a great conviction. We grow dull and stale and unproductive when we limit ourselves to the four walls of our studies. Our messages grow uninteresting, they lack appeal when they grow out of a too-cloistered life. Probably we never rise to such heights of power as when we are made righteously indignant at conditions that have deeply stirred our emotions. Lincoln's Emancipation Proclamation might not have been written had he not witnessed the sale of a slave girl, offered on the block as a human chattel. It was then the fire was kindled in his soul and he set himself the mighty task of destroying this evil. Mr. Beecher was roused by the ungenerous course of England when she wilfully misjudged the motives of the North in a civil strife. Never did he rise to greater heights of power and burning eloquence than when challenged by the angry mobs that would not yield to his persuasion until he had lashed them with his fiery tongue. There is a form of righteous anger that is justified on occasion. It found expression when with stern condemnation and knotted whipcords the gentle Master drove the hucksters and traffickers from temple precincts.

Go out into your world, brush elbows with the crowd, feel its rapid pulse and catch something of its hot temper; know men and women, know their problems, their struggles, their temptations and their sins, then while the fires burn make ready your message and have no fear of the face of man. Jesus prayed for his disciples, "Not that Thou shouldst take them out of the world, but keep them from the evil of the world." His own ministry is the high and holy standard we are called to emulate. His touch with life was immediate and intimate. He walked in the ways of common men. He met fishermen at their nets and called them to be fishers of men. He found the despised publican at his receipt of custom and bade him follow Him. There was nothing ascetic about Him, and so closely did He follow the paths of our workaday experience that "the common people heard Him gladly." He knew what was in men because He companioned with them. His messages were strewn along the open highway. He literally went out into the byways and hedges, seeking that which was lost. He discovered men and women to themselves, reviving in them their forgotten virtues.

What a ministry was His! Does our world want such a ministry to-day, nay is it not eager for it? Our assignment as ambassadors is one of transcendant importance and privilege. We are not ambassadors to foreigners and strangers, not to a limited few, not to some highly chosen and elect, but to all men, everywhere. Be it in obscure hamlet or village, or in town or teeming city, ours is a commission that empowers us for a service of the highest and holiest ends. That is a fine passage from the gifted pen of John Morley:

> We cannot, like Beethoven or Handel, lift the soul by the magic of divine melody into the seventh heaven of ineffable vision and hope incommensurable; we cannot, like Newton, weigh the far-off stars in a balance, and measure the heavings of the eternal flood; we cannot, like Voltaire, scorch up what is cruel and false by a word as a flame, nor like Milton or Burke, awaken men's hearts with the note of an organ-trumpet; we cannot, like the great saints of the churches and the great sages of the schools, add to those acquisitions of spiritual beauty and intellectual mastery which have, one by one and little by little, raised man from being no higher than the brute to be only a little lower than the angels. But what we can do (the humblest of us) is, by diligently seeking to extend our own opportunities to others, to help to swell that common tide, on the force and the set of whose currents depends the prosperous voyaging of humanity.

What greater challenge is offered to men than that of being spokesman for Christ? Ambassadors, clothed with authority, to make Him known to all men, everywhere. When Moses was called to his large duty to speak for God in behalf of an enslaved people, you recall that he sought to withdraw from so mighty a task. "Who am I, that I should go to Pharaoh?" In the hour of his bewilderment, God admonished him to use his brother Aaron as the voice eloquent; and to give him assurance of the greatness of his responsibility, he was given this further solemn word of direction, "Thou shall be to him instead of God." In some way he was to embody the authority of God to his brother, to be the human instrumentality by which divine power was to be transmitted. It was a tremendous task and an incomparable obligation that was laid upon him.

That you and I are set to such a high and solemn duty, must fill us with a sense of profound humility and at the same time thrill us with a consciousness of the greatness of our privilege. What dignity, what power it implies, "Thou shalt be to thy brother; as in the place of God."

Be God's revealer to him, be God's voice speaking to him, be, let us say it with chastened lips, a life saver, Christ's minister plenipotentiary. What need, what indescribable need there is, dear brethren, for this type of ministry to-day; how the world yearns for and responds to such a messenger bearing such a message; the man clothed with his Lord's authority and power.

It was said of one that "he ran so close with the sun,

that men could tell what time of day it was by looking in his face." Not to tell of the passing time of fleeting days, no not this be our privilege, but to tell men of a timeless life, a life of high fulfillment, a life that is an "eternal becoming." It can, it must be done; yes, done by men who will count not their lives dear unto themselves until He is made regnant, until every knee shall bow to his scepter, and every tongue confess, that he is Lord—to the

Glory of God the Father.

CHAPTER IV

HIS EQUIPMENT

One of the blessed and most profitable things that accrues to such a gathering as this, is what it develops in us of the love of comradeship.

Our differences grow largely out of our insularity, our habits of proud isolation. The divisive influences that work such havoc among us come largely from our enforced practice of detachment. We readily find the ground of our agreement when we sit together to consider our common problems, the problems of our common ministry. When Silas Marner had, through misfortune, lost touch with the world about him and become a recluse, his heart was steeled and his nature became coldly repellent. We may be bitter controversialists in the loneliness of our studies, we hardly dare to be such when we have fellowship one with another. Here in such a genial atmosphere as this, we may say with the pilgrims on the road to Emmaus, "did not our hearts burn within us, as He talked with us by the way." The world in which we live is busy at its tasks; selfishness, greed, indifference, unrestrained indulgence, contempt for ideals, these on the one hand; generosity, selflessness, restraint, devotion to all that is best and noblest, these on the other, constitute the arena of action in which we play our part. What we may contribute through our ministry to reconcile the seeming irreconcilable, to make the indifferent, different, to make the ignoble, noble, in fine, to make Christ evident to men, so that they shall acknowledge His sovereignty and be obedient to His will, this we affirm is the task to which we resolutely set ourselves. We believe we have a mission that is indispensable to the attainment of satisfaction and abiding peace; we affirm anew our willingness to lay all that we have on the altar of His service; we accept our assignment in the full confidence of our essential oneness and unity in Him, and we address ourselves again to a fresh appraisal of our equipment. There are many new devices, many modern inventions that a modern and capricious age presents for our consideration. The absorbing question which each one is called upon to decide for himself, is whether he is so equipped that he can meet, and meet effectively, the pressing and crowding needs which his office is compelled to reckon with and to consider.

Within comparatively recent years there has been developed in the capital of the nation a school of diplomacy. This school is designed to prepare and equip men for the arduous task the government lays upon them when sending them to foreign nations. The obvious effect of such training is readily disclosed in the improved conditions of our diplomatic and consular service, fitting men to deal with intricate problems, developing in them courtesy, tact, and forbearance. Not alone does it greatly increase their efficiency, but it renders them more acceptable to the governments to which they are accredited. The results that have accrued to this more modern method have lifted the standards of our diplomatic and consular service to new levels of importance and dignity.

The study of languages and history, of political and economic questions is obviously important. We have come to believe, however, that this study must be supplemented and enriched by a more thorough training in the niceties and refinements that make for gentility and courtesy in all the relationships of life. We have proven by long experience that, in maintaining right and amicable relations with our world neighbors, our chosen representatives must possess certain qualities of mind and heart. Our colleges and seminaries are supposed to accomplish precisely the same results, in equipping men for the duties and responsibilities of their ministry, in the field of service to which they are commissioned. We doubt not that this training does equip men intellectually, preparing them to deal intelligently with many of the problems of parochial life.

That the seminary student is given a theory concerning the functions and purposes of the ministry is quite obvious. This we readily admit. Based upon a study of theology, history, polity, system, organization, and other kindred and related subjects, the student goes forth to his unknown and untried field of activity, there to experiment with the theories he has learned in the classroom. In the main, he has no so-called clinical experience. Unlike the young doctor, he has not served his term as an interne in a hospital. Unlike the law student, he has had no experience in the practical details of his office, nor the more valued experience of an apprenticeship that this profession demands before admitting him to practice at the bar.

As one of the so-called learned professions, our system is singularly deficient in this respect. We literally take a man of small and indifferent experience and untested ability and consign him to a field, there to work out not only the salvation of the souls committed to his care, but his own salvation as well. With comparatively little knowledge of parochial administration, and with possibly less knowledge concerning the purpose and importance of his preaching ministry, with still less experience in the use of his great textbook, we commit him to a task, the problems and difficulties of which, all too frequently, embarrass and overwhelm him.

Very often these young crusaders experience in their early ministry, disillusionment and disappointment, through the realization that they lack certain elements that constitute equipment, an equipment that neither their college nor seminary courses gave them. Plunged into the active duties of parochial life, they speedily find themselves unprepared to meet its large and pressing issues. This is more particularly true as it applies to the pastoral and prophetic aspects of the Christian ministry.

The last thing which the average divinity student seems to know is how to deal with individual souls, how to bring refreshment and stimulation to those who have met with disappointment and failure, or whose faith has been impaired, if not shattered, through mishap or misfortune. In the exercise of the prophetic ministry, to know what to preach, and how to preach, causes confusion and embarrassment to the man whose training has taken insufficient cognizance of this important office.

Meeting with disappointment and seeming failure at the very outset, many a young clergyman becomes disheartened and discouraged, thus losing confidence in his ability to carry the burdens he has assumed. In such a situation, with a growing sense of loneliness, it takes something of the heroic to prosecute a task for which he seems so ill prepared. The studies upon which he spent his longest hours, do not stand him in stead when the testing time comes. The limitations of college and seminary training grow more conspicuous as one studies the Church's situation to-day.

That was a fine admonition which the great apostle gave to his young son, Timothy, "Study to show thyself approved unto God, a workman that needeth not to be ashamed." In this word of counsel he placed the ministry on the highest level. Beyond all else, Timothy was to seek to have the consciousness of divine favor and approval. With such divine favor and approval, he would stand before men unabashed and unashamed.

After all there is something more needed than that which the college and seminary can give. It is that which a man has and cultivates within himself. It has been said that a man gets out of life what he puts into it. If this be true of other occupations and professions, it is preëminently true of the ministry. If ever a man is the architect of his own fortunes, it is in this high and holy calling. If the divinity student feels, with the end of his seminary course in sight, that his arduous and laborious studies are over, he is beginning a career that can have but one issue, namely, failure.

Observation does not lead us to believe that the average divinity student or indeed, the average minister, is troubled over-much with an inferiority complex. On the other hand, it is evident that too many seem to lack a clear understanding of their highest potentiality. They set for themselves too low an ideal or standard of excellence. The highest self-development lays a costly toll upon us. To be what we ought to be, means study, discipline and self-imposed sacrifice.

A cross was a terrible price to pay for Saviourhood, yet the Master paid it, declaring: "I, if I be lifted up, will draw all men unto me."

We recall the instance of a man conspicuous in the ministry, who in the middle of his rather notable career, told a divinity student that he had not read a new book or prepared a new sermon for a period of ten years. It would not be difficult to determine this man's place of power and influence. His is a case of arrested mental and spiritual growth. He was spending his principal recklessly, when he ought to have been living on his accrued interest.

To the latest hour of our active service we must be seeking new and fresh equipment. This equipment differs largely from that which is required in other professions and callings. It is designed to serve different ends and purposes. To the militant mind of St. Paul, it was in the nature of an armor. Writing to the young Christian converts in Ephesus, he said:

> Put on the whole armour of God, that ye may be able to withstand in the evil day, and having done all to stand.

There is something singularly striking and graphic in his description of this equipment.

> Stand, therefore, having your loins girt about with truth, and having on the breastplate of righteousness, and your feet shod with the preparation of the gospel of peace; above all, taking the shield of faith wherewith ye shall be able to quench all the fiery darts of the wicked; and take the helmet of salvation and the sword of the spirit, which is the word of God.

Such equipment rendered the disciple competent to wrestle against flesh and blood, against principalities, against powers, against the rulers of the darkness of this world, against spiritual wickedness in high places.

It is obvious that the ideal of service that the apostle here sets forth, contemplates an aggressive, persistent and continuing warfare against the forces of evil. It is something that appeals to the heroic within each one of us. The armor is obviously complete in all its parts, it has every essential demanded by the situation. All this we readily recognize, but we may not forget that, while this is an equipment that is absolutely perfect, it demands a virile and consecrated manhood behind it to render it efficient and worthy of use. Says a distinguished student of human affairs, "It is not so much by pens as by personalities, that God sets the world forward." This brings us to the heart of what we have in mind to discuss, namely, the indispensableness of a highly developed personality.

Very frequently men who have lacked large training

and cultural gifts have rendered a service of incomparable value to the Christian cause. They possessed elements of strength, intellectual and spiritual qualities, that gave them preëminence and power in this holy calling. While they may have lacked some of the things we regard as indispensable to a well-rounded professional career, they had that which gave them a place of commanding power and influence.

We speak of such men as being gifted with what we call "personal magnetism." It is a term which it is difficult to define, and is descriptive of that which is still more difficult of attainment. While this rare gift may differ in degree in varying types of men, we are profoundly convinced that it is susceptible of cultivation and development. It is very difficult to define what constitutes genius. It is still more difficult to define what constitutes the power of personality. While we believe that some men are born with rare gifts and qualities that lead them to heights of power, we have abundant examples of other men, less gifted, who have been able through persistent application and exacting preparation to so prepare and equip themselves that they came at length to occupy places of large distinction and usefulness. As we come to study their careers, we note first that they were primarily and essentially natural. In other words, they were true to that which was peculiarly their own. There was nothing artificial or unreal about them. They preserved in themselves that which belonged to their type of individuality.

We know of no profession that calls for more of naturalness than the one in which we are engaged. We know of no place where a man should be more truly himself than in the exercise of his office in the sanctuary. Nothing is more repellent and indeed reprehensible in the conduct of corporate worship, or in the preaching of the eternal gospel, than a borrowed or assumed habit or method, entirely foreign to the man who uses it. A fine word for every one of us in this connection is the one that Polonius gave his son Laertes, namely, "to thine own self be true."

The borrowed raiment or habit of another proves ill-fitting, unadorning and unsatisfactory. David could not wear Saul's armor. We have known men, who in their search for distinction, attempted to reproduce the rapid utterance of a Phillips Brooks, or the unctuous and more measured style of a Theodore Cuyler. We have known others who in their mad search for originality of style attempted to simulate the extraordinary eccentricities of those whose novel and unique ways won for them a place of peculiar distinction and popularity. Again, we have known still others to indulge in the careless style or habit of dress, which was characteristic of some strikingly original thinker. Such cheap imitation savors of weakness and mental ineptitude.

I think it will be readily admitted that the true function and high purpose of education is to develop in a man his true personality. A modern writer of large vision has lately asserted that our system of education as it obtains to-day, is singularly defective in this respect; that instead of cultivating and developing the personality of the student, it tends to impair it by offering it a dozen substitutes.

It is unquestionably true that so potent and compelling are the influences of academic and seminary life that all too frequently the mind loses its own self-assertiveness and initiative, as it falls a victim to the norms or standards that are prescribed and set for it. The uniformity of class instruction, the indespensableness of prescribed textbooks, the daily routine that must of necessity be fixed and formal, all these have a tendency to make the student more or less mechanical, and unless he is singularly resourceful, deprive him of those qualities of mind and heart that are distinctly his own.

We observe the evidence of all this in much of our pulpit ministry to-day. The similarity of style and manner, the widespread use of a tone of expression in the conduct of corporate worship, and even in preaching, the stilted and formal methods in approach to individuals, whether in the sanctuary or out of it, all these witness to the undue influence of a too precise and formal method of training that subordinates the student's personality, rendering it artificial and unresponsive to what are peculiarly and uniquely his own gifts and qualities of mind and heart. Some one has aptly said, "We are born originals and die copies."

We are not stressing the claims of eccentricity or idiosyncrasy, we are not seeking to maintain that the prescribed curriculum of the classroom must undergo revolutionary changes. The value of precision and orderliness in the training of divinity students is imperatively demanded. As a matter of fact, we believe we would have a finer ministry to-day in the Christian Church, were the disciplines of the seminary more precise and exacting than they are.

The whole point we are insisting upon is that, in all our training and reading, in all our administrative work and preaching, we should ever seek to preserve that which we have discovered within ourselves to be God's peculiar gift to us. Kant expresses it when he says, "The aim of education is to give the individual all the perfection of which he is capable."

A ministry of one type and kind, whose ways and practices are prescribed by some dogmatic manual, must come at length to make the Christian Church an ineffective instrumentality in serving the high purposes for which it was designed. Our Lord Himself acknowledged the wide difference in the ministry of John, the Forerunner, and that which He himself exemplified, and yet He declared that "there had not been born of woman a greater than John."

The differences in that early apostolic body were marked and great. So marked, indeed, that one of the sharpest contentions recorded in the New Testament was that between St. Peter and St. Paul concerning the emphases of their ministry. The greatest reformations that have stirred, aroused and awakened whole continents have been ushered in by men who refused to sink their own personalities and individualities, or to make them subordinate to some dominant and autocratic machine.

The evidences in the history of the Christian Church for the contention we are making, are abundant and convincing. The most dynamic and progressive periods in its history, have been promoted and led by men whose glowing personalities excelled all the agencies and mechanisms with which they had to do. "The spirit of the living creature was in the wheels." These heroic figures are like Himalayan peaks soaring high above their less aspiring and persevering comrades. It was Bishop Westcott who maintained that the growing, yes, and the glowing, periods in the Church's life were not those where it was dominated by the classroom, or made conformable to the precise dictum of its scholars. They were the periods that were distinguished by the rise of men, men of great spiritual stature, who dared to assert and to maintain the high principles of life, of which they themselves were the embodiment and expression. Their ways may not have been the ways of a rigid conformity, and their utterances may have done violence to that which tradition had prescribed, and yet their voices had persuasive and compelling power. Theirs was not a case of exaggerated ego, it was rather one that witnessed to the fulfillment of a high and holy purpose, to which they believed they had been singularly and strangely commissioned. Matthew Arnold in his poem, "Self-dependence," describes such, and the secret of their strength:

> Bounded by themselves, and unregardful
> In whatsoever state God's other works may be,
> In their own tasks all their powers pouring,
> These attain the mighty life you see.
>
> O air born voice! long since severely clear,
> A cry like thine in mine own heart I hear:
> Resolve to be thyself, and know, that he,
> Who finds himself, loses his misery.

Let us remember always that true apostolic power

ever belongs to the lineage of apostolically minded men. It is inevitably true that in no period of the world's history has God left Himself without witnesses; and these mighty witnesses, let us never forget, have been those who before all else, were captains of their own souls. They have been the beacon lights of the Christian Church. Indeed, they have been the trail-makers for our advancing civilization. The luminous examples of those we have in mind are too many to be named here.

The most vital and pregnant periods in the story of the Church's history and development are associated with individuals who possessed within themselves the sources of their genius and power. It is hard to classify such men. It is difficult to say to what cult or party they belong. Catholic-minded, they refuse to be limited in their sphere of service; they repudiate passwords and shibboleths that bespeak a fellowship restricted and circumscribed.

If in other days the Church made its greatest advance under men of this type and character; if experience has shown that the periods of marked progress in the life of the Church have been characterized by leaders of this kind, then surely the age in which we live is demanding the emulation of their virtues and a freshened exhibition of their courage. As we survey the work done by men of this heroic mold, we readily forget the type of churchmanship they represented, or the form of organization under which they served.

A single modern example will serve our purpose. One of the most outstanding and conspicuous figures of the World War was the cardinal whose superb and heroic defense of the people committed to his charge arrested and commanded the admiration of men the world over. Possibly no figure that looms on the horizons of this great struggle is more commanding and compelling than Cardinal Mercier. That he was the accredited prince of a great church and one of its chosen counselors, did not affect the judgment of the world in appraising his worth, or giving him a place of highest distinction among its outstanding and chosen leaders. The color of his robe or the fashion of his speech sink into insignificance, as we appraise the moral grandeur of his character. Greater than any authority conferred upon him by his church, was that which he carried in his own person. He was the chosen guardian of a people's sacred rights; a high priest, who held his commission from the pierced hands of his divine Master.

Such a man seems greater than any organization, however highly and efficiently conceived it may be. The whole world renders him its homage, and acknowledges his priestly authority. We recall in our own day and generation the universal expressions of sorrow when Phillips Brooks lay dead in the church in which he had with matchless eloquence preached to countless thousands. So great was his power in Boston that when his body was borne from the church that he had rendered famous, a vast multitude gathered in Copley Square, representing every type and phase of churchmanship, acknowledged him as their leader, and with one voice proclaimed him their bishop.

You and I in our day and generation will come to our place of power and influence, not so much because of the distinctions that have been conferred upon us as for that which we in our own persons represent and incarnate.

The large question that must command our deepest consideration is, have we within us potentialities, gifts or powers, that are susceptible of development? Has God given to each one of us certain things, talents if you will, that are peculiarly our own, the recognition and use of which constitute our unique contribution to life. No discovery we ever make is comparable to that which we make concerning ourselves.

As a matter of fact, the significance of all the later discoveries in life is affected by the discovery of our own mental gifts and aptitudes. When once we have come to know the meaning of our own soul, when once we have determined for ourselves what is the high purpose of our being, we have risen to an eminence where we are able to survey the new land of promise. With such self-revelation, we are able to determine by what methods and processes we may attain our highest fulfillment. The old classic maxim, "Know thyself," has a deep and significant meaning.

One of the striking things in the ministry of Jesus is his discovery to men of their forgotten selves. He surprised men, as in the case of Nathaniel, by the accuracy of his knowledge. He uncovered in lives that seemed sterile and barren, talents and virtues that had long lain dormant and inactive. Under the winsomeness of His compelling love, natures that seemed harsh and forbidding were softened, and made responsive to the call of noble impulses and high ideals. There is that within each one of us that responds to this divine call. The very expectancy of Jesus, His utter hopefulness concerning us, brings to fruition and useful service the finer and better things of our nature.

In this process of self-revelation, that I hold to be indispensable to a well-rounded and highly developed and efficient service in the ministry, we shall doubtless gain much by a study of the great masters who have gone before us.

If the artist and the musician find themselves enriched and profited by long and laborious study of the masters of their professions, surely we may find like profit and enrichment by a continued and unbroken study of the men who have excelled in the ministry. We do not study them in order that we may reproduce their style, nor yet their peculiarities and eccentricities. We may consistently study them in order to reveal to our consciousness what constituted the secret of their genius and the elements of their persuasive powers. Much reading is no guarantee of a finished style—much thinking is. Not many masters, but a few truly great ones, contribute to our mental and spiritual growth and enrichment.

We recall the incident of the young student in Phillips Brooks' library who, while waiting for the great preacher, began a cursory examination of the books that lined his shelves. Upon entering the room and greeting the expectant youth, the prophet said to him, "Are you looking for some special book?" "No," he responded, "I am trying to discover the secret of your genius and power." "You will not find it," said the preacher, "by studying the backs of the books in my library." There was something naïve about the young man's search for the preacher's distinction.

The young artist does not gain much in the way of technical skill by studying a gallery of some individual artist's pictures. He does gain power and talent by studying the notable examples of the men of genius of varying types.

We have often been struck with the lack of knowledge of the great prophets disclosed by those who are pursuing day by day and week by week the art of pastoral and prophetic work. A too great indulgence in the study of the style of one single master may prove harmful to us. It may produce that meanest and most despicable of all pulpit defects, namely, imitation. On the other hand, a wide reading and study of men of varying types and gifts does have a tendency to stimulate within us freshened ambitions and aspirations, and to compel us to finer efforts after achievement.

Speaking from personal experience, I have found infinite profit in studying the master stylists of the pulpit, not merely reading their sermons and noting their powers of expression, but in studying their lives. One need not, nor ought he to be confined to master-preachers alone, he ought to pursue unremittingly a study of the great masters of expression. I recall an observation made to me by one of the notable preachers of a former generation. He said: "Read for your intellectual profit only the masters of the best English." "English," he continued, "is the medium through which you are to express your thoughts, therefore, you must read only the best, else your own style will betray the evidences of an impoverished and unreplenished mind, your vocabulary will prove inadequate to your needs. Read and study the great poets, they were artists, they stimulate the imagination and enrich the mind. Spend a portion of each day in the presence of a great soul." Surely such a recommendation needs no endorsement or emphasis.

It was said of Lincoln that he read but few books. The Bible, Shakespeare and Bunyan were his constant companions, and from the careful study of these he became such a master of English that his notable utterances have come to be regarded as classics.

Here again may we be warned of the dangers of borrowing the equipment of another. The only value of the study we are commending lies in the freshened stimulation it affords, in bringing to their highest and most effective development our own gifts and qualities of mind and heart. "Stir up the gift that is in thee," was the admonition of the apostle to the young man who was his son in the faith. He was not asking him to reproduce the virtues of his own militant ministry. He was rather seeking to compel him to a process of self-revelation, in order to develop and bring forth latent gifts and qualities that seemed dormant and inactive.

Unlike other notable professions, you and I have one supreme master to whom we are compelled to turn, as the great exemplar of the high things of our profession.

As we study the amazing and almost miraculous ministry of those early peasant disciples, we are compelled to realize that they possessed unusual gifts, and employed certain unique methods, that must have come to them in ways worthy of our deep and serious consideration. It was said of them that they had "been with Jesus and learned of Him."

That there was an extraordinary development in the life of a Peter, a John or a James, and that without a background of careful training they were enabled to do a work and to effect results that find no parallel in the subsequent history of the Church, is clearly evident. What genius or power so stirred the heart and mind of St. Peter that he had as an immediate result of one sermon the conversion of three thousand souls?

The whole story of the early development of the Christian Church is one that finds nothing comparable to it in its later growth and development. Only in those periods that have been marked by a similar zeal and a like high consecration, have we witnessed anything approximating the conquest of this early period. To discover the secret of it, is our supreme quest. The prophets in succeeding generations, who have measurably reached up to the power and influence of this early Church, have ever been those who have caught their inspiration from this same divine Master, whom these early disciples so loyally and faithfully followed.

Again, the periods that have been marked by sterility and a devitalized church, have been those where its chosen leaders failed to sit at the feet of Him who spake as never man spake. One of the most remarkable things that the casual observer is bound to note in our world of to-day, is the fact that the sheer popularity of Jesus, instead of declining, grows with unabated power and force. Where critics generous and ungenerous, censure the Church for its lack of progressiveness, its seeming incapacity to keep step with the life of the age, they invariably acknowledge the sovereignty and regnancy of Christ, and despite their defection from the Church, pay homage to Him as Lord and Master.

If the "originality of Jesus," as someone has said, amazes us, surely His persistence in human thought, and His continuing and unabated influence down through the centuries, must be regarded as one of the conspicuous evidences of His divine mission.

When in our more introspective moods (and they can never be too frequent) we seek to discover the indispensable things of our equipment, surely we must find that nothing we have or have received is remotely comparable to that which we have gleaned from long and persistent study of the life of the Master Himself. Self-discovery must mean Christ discovery, and Christ discovery must issue in a fuller self-discovery. If those to whom we essay to minister do not realize that we have companioned with Him, and that our inspiration and power proceed from Him, surely our ministry must fail of large results.

It was away from the world of stern competitions and intense action that Jesus repeatedly withdrew His disciples, and it was on such occasions that He disclosed to them the high purpose of His ministry. It was only when Peter declared in his great confession his belief in the sovereignty and divinity of Christ that he was invested with a new power and commissioned to a service of high accomplishment. It was in places of retirement that Jesus made the largest disclosures of Himself, and almost invariably it was to lonely individuals. What He had to say and give, seemed to require detachment from the world.

Dr. Whitehead suggestively says: "True religion is solitariness, and if you are never solitary, you are never religious." Can we in our present-day ministry believe that strenuous living and an excess of indulgence in parochial and other activities, unaccompanied by protracted periods in the silences, where we stand face to face with our divine Lord as well as face to face with the realities of life, will develop in us that kind of equipment that makes for real efficiency, and guarantees to us the lasting results of our service?

Be certain of this, unless we can in some-wise approximate the vision of life disclosed in the ministry of our Lord, unless we can in some-wise catch His conception of the value of the human soul, we shall find our ministry to men seriously embarrassed, if not hopelessly impaired. If personal magnetism occupies a large place, especially in our pulpit ministry, if there is an effluence that proceeds from us that mightily affects those to whom we minister, it is augmented with an irresistible power when men discover that it has the Christ dynamic behind it.

To be able to say, "I live, yet not I, but Christ liveth in me," is to so enhance and empower our ministry that it becomes indescribably appealing and fruitful. There is a subtle influence that proceeds from us that either draws men to our side, or drives them from us. It is the incarnation of our creed, the witness of our faith, the secret of our hope, the evidence of our authority. To climb the pulpit stairs with a life that is written over with characters of wholesome truth, is better than to have the eloquence of a golden-mouthed Chrysostom. The personality in the pulpit is the centrifugal force in the Church, the sun in its solar system.

A congregation moves about within the limitations of its orbit, and feels the impelling and compelling power of the one from whom it has its light and heat. The magnetic influence toward which the needle of public favor ever turns, and by whose supreme power it is governed, is the consecrated, God-empowered man. "I am the voice of one," declared the Forerunner, and in this we discover the secret of his power. It is safe to say that there has been no great preacher who has given men an inspiration to live, who has not infused into his every utterance something of his own divinely gifted personality. It takes a week of manly preparation to produce a manly sermon, a week of manly prayer to faithfully present the manly man, Christ Jesus.

We sometimes talk about the waning interest in the gospel story, the waning interest in the Church. Let us not forget that it was waning in Florence when the master of St. Mark's was heard, challenging a state for its sins; it was waning in England when Wycliffe and Latimer and Ridley and Wesley called it from its supineness; it was waning in the Colonies when Edwards and Whitefield stirred it from its lethargy and inaction.

These mighty prophets came with their equipment, but it was something more than the equipment which the classroom had given them. Their authority was something more than that which had been conferred by ordaining hands. Their word was with convincing power, because in themselves they had experienced not only the love of Him who had a passion for souls, but the glowing influence of that divine life with which they had daily companioned. They could truly say: "The love of Christ constraineth me."

Entirely apart from all else that they represented, they were the flaming heralds of a living Savior of men.

What did Jesus mean in that profound utterance where He said, "He that loseth his life, shall find it?" Surely this, that only as we subordinate our life to His life, only as we make our wills obedient to His will, are we able to discover the divinity within us. "He must increase, but I must decrease," said John the Baptist. It was through self-abdication he would realize the meaning of a Christ-empowered life. Arrogance and pride and self-confidence, yes, and our conceit of orders, all these must we yield to Him. He must increase, but we must decrease.

Poor, boastful men that we are, we come to believe that with our mighty wisdom or little wit, we are capable of ushering in the kingdom of God on earth, of making His temple so splendid, so refreshing, so exhilarating that multitudes shall be drawn to it. We bring our culture, our refinement, our excess of learning and lay them upon the altar of service, and then wonder why the flame is not kindled, why the sacrifice is not honored. Our splendid equipment gets small response because it lacks certain elements that are indispensable. Our very utterance betrays the lack of calm, our unfamiliarity with long periods spent in deep reflection and prayer. We seem to forget that "as

He prayed the fashion of His countenance was altered," that divine as He was, His face was made luminous and resplendent as He communed with the eternal Father.

The modern prophet or leader who isolates himself in the mount of spiritual vision, who shuts out for the while the voices of the world, even the quiet voices of the mighty ones, must come to a waiting people with something that speaks in no uncertain way of a transformed and transfigured life. The world is quick to recognize and acknowledge the light that suggests divine illumination, and no artificial, ephemeral brilliance may ever take its place. The rich acquisitions of culture and learning will hardly be admitted as substitutes for this strange power, the power that glowed in the eyes and uttered its message through the lips of Jesus Christ. Let us not forget that it was while assembled in the silent chamber of devotion, waiting for they knew not what, that a band of peasants experienced the illuminating power of the Pentecostal flame.

Every renewal of this miraculous power has come through some personality, whose flaming zeal has been enkindled through contact with the Master life. Every true and lasting revival of Christian faith, every advance of the Christian Church, has been distinguished by this same kind of leadership.

You and I will give ourselves betimes to much reading and thinking, we will diligently follow the methods of a modern and progressive church, but as we come more and more to understand the deep needs of the world, and our relation to them, we will be compelled to seek for our inspiration at the feet of Him who alone has brought life and immortality to light. To plead daily for our nobler self-hood, to struggle after the attainment of that which is Godlike within us, to realize in some degree the expression of our better and truer nature, means to walk at length with Him who treads amid the golden candlesticks.

A personality that like some beneficent influence brings refreshment and inspiration to a disillusioned world, that leaves behind a trail of light, that gives the tired soul its peace, the cloudy noon its sun, is the personality that from its oft-repeated communings with the Master rises to duties that await, with strength renewed, with soul aflame, with life ordained. So beautiful and pervasive was the Christian character of his son that Charles Wagner, the French preacher, wrote this word concerning him at the time of his death: "Thou hast sown with rays of white light the pathway to the grave, and left at the gates of death a gleam as of dawn."

Masefield in one of his strikingly suggestive passages thus sums up the greatness and the glory of personality, consciously awake to its high and holy privileges:

> Here in the self is all that man can know
> Of beauty, all the wonder, all the power,
> All the unearthly color, all the glow,
> Here in the self which withers like a flower;
> Here in the flesh, within the flesh, behind,
> Swift in the blood and throbbing on the bone,
> The God, the Holy Ghost, the atoning Lord,
> Here in the flesh, the never yet explored.

CHAPTER V

HIS LOYALTIES

I have attempted in an earlier lecture to give emphasis to the important question of fitness, the fitness of the man for his mission. There can be no word too urgent given to those who seek the ministry, bearing upon this primary matter. So definite is the mind of an ancient Church here that in its ordinal it asks of each candidate the searching question: "Do you think in your heart, that you are truly called, according to the will of our Lord Jesus Christ?" and further: "Will you be diligent to form and fashion your own self and your family, according to the doctrine of Christ; and make both yourself and them, as much as in you lieth, wholesome examples and patterns to the flock of Christ?"

These solemn words must make a highly conscientious man search his own heart, and lay upon him a deepened sense of his responsibility. It compels him once again, before the great step is taken, to discover afresh both his fitness and his worthiness. It ought to be obvious that, in his own mind, the question of a "call to service" is settled once and forever.

What then is the cause that challenges his wholehearted endeavor? There can be but one answer, it is to fulfill John the Forerunner's ideal concerning his ministry: "That He should be made manifest, therefore am I come." He is not so much committed to a system as to a cause. Systems and methods may fail, but the cause, never. It is a cause that renders his office different from all other worldly occupations and professions; more urgent, more pressing, more fascinating. Its sphere of action is coterminous with human life the world over. Its metes and bounds are without limit; its ultimate design is the redemption of men from the bondage of sin; its seemingly impossible task is to create here on earth a condition so completely in accord with the mind of Christ, that all men shall recognize His sovereignty and be obedient to His will. It literally means, let us be clear about it, an effort to create "a new earth, wherein dwelleth righteousness."

Such a mighty task calls for more of genius than that which the gifted statesman displays; more of courage than is exhibited by the leader of a militant host. It is a great and fascinating adventure.

We can readily understand how a man may assume the weighty obligations of other callings and subsequently change his opinions concerning them, and possibly determine to alter his course. This is frequently done. It is conceivable that a man may too hastily enter upon a career and later revise his views concerning it; it is hardly conceivable, with the exacting and rigorous preparation demanded of him who essays the office of the ministry, that he will hold his obligations so lightly as to regard himself as immune to their solemn implications. True, a changed conviction or the discovery of inaptitude may compel a man to renounce his office and seek for a new field of service.

When done with sincerity and without ulterior motive, such a transition may be unchallengeable. Ralph Waldo Emerson is a striking example of what we have in mind.

On the other hand, to retain this office in the face of altered convictions, impelled by a selfish desire to receive its honors and emoluments, while repudiating its assumed obligations, is wholly indefensible and reprehensible. It is true that when this lectureship was established some fifty-seven years ago, the Church and indeed the ministry itself were confronted with conditions wholly and widely different from those we face to-day. Old molds of thought, old habits, practices and conventions seemed to be fixed and unchanging. The routine of ministerial service, the unchallenged ancient formularies of the Church, the fixed interpretation of creeds, a rigid adherence to time-honored customs and age-old traditions, all these held their unchallenged and undisputed place. In the light of modern thought and practice some among us might be compelled to say with Paul, as they view these ancient landmarks: "After the way which they call heresy, so worship I the God of my fathers."

Admitting all this, let us further acknowledge that there must be, of necessity, some definite, basic and fixed standards of belief, some enduring principles upon which the fabric of the Church as an institution is founded.

I am not for a moment assuming, that this venerable institution is static, that it does not change its methods and practices to meet new and changed conditions. I hold as firmly as another that, flexibility and adaptation of methods to meet new conditions are indispensable. The failure of the Church to do this has repeatedly cost it both prestige and power.

What we are claiming, and we dare not claim less, is that, looseness of belief, or worse still, an indifferent regard to assumed obligations, a sense of freedom, or if you will, license to depart from the Church's established and tested and irreducible minimum of belief, is an offense that brings dishonor and shame to the man who indulges in it.

The time to weigh obligations is when we assume them. An officer or enlisted man who has sworn allegiance to flag and country, may not, as caprice or personal convenience dictate, ignore or abandon his pledged obedience. He may be out of harmony with his exacting environment, he may find that the severe tests of the field prove unappealing and repellent; yes, he may dislike those who have authority over him. It's not his privilege even to "reason why," nor again is it his right to "make reply." He is a sworn servant of his nation and if need be he "must do and die" for the cause to which he is committed.

Josiah Royce in his splendid lectures on the *Philosophy of Loyalty*, has a chapter entitled, "Loyalty to Loyalty," in which he stresses the supreme need of loyalty to a cause. He says: "In choosing and serving the cause to which you are to be loyal, be, in any case, loyal to loyalty." In his mind the cause to which we are committed transcends everything. In maintaining it, personal convenience or the satisfaction of selfish desires and ambitions find no place.

You recall his memorable illustration of the speaker

of the House of Commons and his declination to accede to the royal mandate. Called upon to identify those who had refused to be amenable to the king's dictum, the speaker said: "Your Majesty, I am the speaker of this House, and, being such, I have neither eyes to see nor tongue to speak, save as this House shall command." Here, says Professor Royce, is a supreme example of loyalty, loyalty to a cause, a cause that rises far above the royal mandate. Well does he add that this is an expression of the "dignity that any loyal man, great or humble, possesses, whenever he speaks and acts in the service of his cause."

That you and I are irrevocably committed to a cause, is clearly evident; with what scrupulous care then must we ever place it above self and selfish interests. Where the cause is jeopardized or its influence in anywise curtailed by our carelessness or unwillingness to defend it, we transgress a cardinal principle that affects, not alone our own moral stability, but the stability and security of the institution whose servants we are.

"Loyalty to Loyalty," is a maxim that must receive unfailing obedience from the servant of Jesus Christ. Let us hear the conclusion of Professor Royce in what he calls his "thesis."

> All those duties which we have learned to recognize as the fundamental duties, the duties that every man owes to every man, are to be rightly interpreted as special instances of loyalty to loyalty. I assert that, when rightly interpreted, loyalty is the whole duty of man. Disloyalty is moral suicide.

HIS LOYALTIES

We have fallen upon a time when the sense of obligation to the body corporate, to the institution, be it the State, the body social or the Church itself, is lightly held and esteemed. Personal liberty is overstressed and overstrained in our day. The opinion and will of the individual is set over against the expressed and lawful opinion and will of the body corporate. This runs the gamut of our whole life. Disobedience to or disregard of law, is taken as an evidence of independence, or even assumed to be an expression of originality.

It's a sorry state of affairs and fraught with grave perils, where the ties of corporate unity are wantonly broken, where orderly procedure is dispossessed and unseated, and individual opinion and so-called personal liberty assume the seat of authority.

Such a situation produces confusion, disorder, and ultimately, anarchy in the State. It does not do less in the Church. Some men delight to convert their pulpit into a laboratory, in which to show their adroitness and cleverness in what might be termed "experimental preaching." They seem to think they win the favor, especially of the intellectual element, when they show their skill in dialectics or their genius for critical analysis. They assume that such an exhibition, while it confuses the multitude, gives them a place of distinction among the more cultivated.

A former distinguished Secretary of State, himself a classical scholar and a student of the Greek text of the New Testament, observed to me not long since that preaching of this sort was emptying the pews of thoughtful, reverent men and women. He found himself wholly out of sympathy with those who made their pulpits debating rostrums or places for the display of their own doubts and speculations. "I am not appealed to or interested," said he, "by what the preacher does not believe, I want to know what he really holds and practices of faith and doctrine." Another scholarly leader in the realm of industry made bold to say that if modern Protestantism had no definiteness of conviction or belief, he would be compelled to abandon his chosen Church, and find refuge in one that, with all its unappealing methods, still stood for something definite and fixed.

The extent of this lay opposition to the looseness and license of the modern pulpit is far more widespread than the clergy themselves seem to realize. There are limits that even this highly protected and sequestered profession may not transgress. If our studies draw us away from the central facts concerning the work and ministry of Jesus, as Master and Savior of men, it were far better that we honestly abandoned our calling and openly disavowed our allegiance to an institution that bears His name.

The world respects one who frankly declares his change of conviction and refuses further distinctions and emoluments from the institution whose ways he can no longer follow. With like ardor, it disrespects, if it does not hold in contempt, another, who violates his pledged faith, and proves disloyal to the recognized standards of a household, in which he essays the rôle of leadership and authority.

The fact that heresy trials are both unpopular and

largely obsolete does not render the bearer of the Church's high commission, immune to its fundamental law and practice. The instance of a clergyman who openly boasted of his disaffection and abandonment of his Church's ways, followed by the bold declaration: "Now try me for heresy, if you dare," is, let us hope, a rare exhibition of the folly in which men will indulge in their bid for cheap notoriety and front-page distinction.

It were far better that the Church declared an "open season," abandoning all time-honored customs and beliefs, renouncing all allegiance to authority, from whatever source or with whatever imprimatur it might come, than that it should give its credentials and accord its privileges to those who repudiate its decrees and do violence to its faith and practice. "If he will not obey her law, neither shall he eat her bread," was the stern but just dictum of one of the most generous and broad-minded leaders the Church has known. He was alluding to one who had openly and defiantly discredited and traduced the teachings of a Church in whose service he held a remunerative and conspicuous place.

A liberal Church we all want; a Church that gives consistent intellectual freedom has been the quest of sincere and honest men for centuries; but let us not do violence to these alluring and appealing terms. To belong to or to attempt to minister in a Church that is so liberal that it has no system, no well-defined order, no fixity of belief or conviction; to enjoy intellectual freedom to such an extent that our faith becomes nebulous, unsatisfying and unassuring, is to stultify and dishonor our office and to render it unacceptable to self-respecting men and women.

I know full well that I am trespassing here upon a field that has advocates, and distinguished ones, of another mind. However, to use the language of the great reformer: "Here I stand, I can do no other, so help me God."

There is nothing in what I have said that is designed to support the fundamentalist on the one hand, or the modernist on the other. We may be consistent fundamentalists in our adherence to the great basic elements of the Christian faith, we may also be open-minded modernists in recognizing what reverent scholarship has done to render more appealing and convincing the ancient canon of scripture. I certainly am no advocate of a restricted ministry, I *am* an advocate of professional honor and honesty, and professional honor is inconceivable without a deep and unfailing sense of loyalty to the institution whose credentials we bear. The situation that is presented in too many places to-day is one that can have but one issue, namely, a discredited ministry and a discredited Church.

The passion for originality, or the still less worthy desire to gain recognition in public press, through eccentricity of utterance, may for a brief space bring satisfaction to the man who indulges in it; it produces at length the utter indifference or silent contempt of those to whom he ministers.

Too many of our religious bodies are built upon foundations laid by one whose insularity of view and practice led him to stress, out of all proportion, some one aspect of Christian teaching. Tolstoi would build his Christian order on a single passage from the Master's great sermon: "Resist not evil." In his *My Religion*, he focuses all upon this single phrase; he would found a new cult upon one great statement, branding as unworthy those who could not and would not accept his dictum.

Our world to-day is filled with the clamorous, strident voices of those who cry their ecclesiastical wares with dogmatic fervor and over-zealous insistence. The tragic story of the unholy rivalries and competitions of institutions that bear the name of Christian, witnesses to the passion of men for that which is novel, bizarre and spectacular. Dr. Whitehead speaks of those "rival pedants who cut out neat little dogmatic systems to serve as the unalterable measure of the universe." Loyalty to the institution is readily abandoned for that which expresses independence of thought and originality of action. To be liberal is esteemed of greater worth than to be consistent.

The eccentricities of individualism lie at the root of much of our present confusion and disorder. We would hesitate to sail the seas with a man who wholly disregarded the well-defined laws of navigation. Latitude and longitude may be arbitrary terms to describe invisible lines, but they have a large meaning and an important bearing upon safe sailing. "Dead reckoning" may be indispensable in foggy weather, but we feel more secure when with sextant and compasses and careful calculation we find our position daily at high noon.

That much of our present Church teaching is based upon "dead reckoning," the reckoning of a pilot whose vision is uncertain and whose atmosphere is clouded, is all too evident. Let us be admonished by that ancient word, "Where there is no vision, the people perish."

That there are basic and fundamental principles that inhere in the Christian Church; that Jesus Christ is the same yesterday, to-day and forever; that history and experience afford convincing and irrefutable proofs as to what is reasonable and valuable and indispensable to the development of Christian character, is demonstrably true. To regard these lightly, to disesteem our responsibility to maintain them, is to prove false to the high trust given us.

Two astute and high-minded manufacturers were discussing in our hearing the present situation in the Church; said one: "We are groping to-day, groping for something that we feel is indispensable to our happiness and peace, and the uncertain note of the modern pulpit is leaving us bewildered and confused. The old message of hope and assurance has been taken from us and we are drifting, with no certainty of our course here and no reasonable assurance of a haven hereafter. Our spiritual guides have lost their way."

They were not men of mediocre intelligence, nor were they of those who refuse to be enlightened. They were quite representative of a vast multitude who to-day are at our altars, insistently demanding bread and not stones. These waiting pilgrims will not be satisfied with the message and ministry of one who holds lightly his allegiance to his high office, or who disesteems his obligations to the Church to which he is accredited.

An ambassador cannot with honor to himself or the cause he represents disown his credentials, or exceed the authority conferred upon him by the institution that sent him forth to an assigned duty and a definite task. Flippancy, or the disclosure of a careless concern for the beauty and deep significance of sacred things, might almost be classified as an unpardonable sin.

Says an astute modern journalist:

> The greatest tragedy in the world is when beautiful things get into the hands of those who do not understand them. The danger is that the most splendid element in human beings, the craving for beauty, for poetry, for worship and ecstasy—in a word, the religious instinct—shall fall into the hands of literal-minded priests, who are eager to crystallize and minify these agencies into small prisms of doctrines.

You may recall Dr. Jowett's grim and caustic word given to Margot Asquith: "You must believe in God, in spite of what the clergy say."

"God may have other words for other worlds, but for this world the word of God is Christ," is the dictum of a distinguished Scotch preacher and author. Our age is characterized, as an outstanding Bishop once said, by a "lust for change and a passion for variety."

We will not run counter to the later disclosures of scientific and scholarly research; we will not close the door upon newer and fresher revelations. We profoundly believe that God is manifesting Himself in new ways to twentieth-century men and women; and that with fine consistency we may bring new interpretations to bear upon old truths. It is your business and mine to keep abreast of modern thought and the man who does not do so, must lose step with his generation. All this we recognize and gladly admit, but we believe and are persuaded that there are principles and truths that are immutable, there are basic facts that inhere in the Christian religion that remain; "nevertheless, the foundation of God standeth sure."

The incarnation of God in Christ, His saviorhood, His redeeming work, His code, if you please, of ethics, still stand. He persists through the ages, in spite of all our so-called conceits of learning; He is as manifest to him who seeks Him to-day as He was to those primitive disciples. We rise to our greatest heights of power when we most clearly identify our life and our message with Him. We are most persuasive and effective, whether in pulpit or in the contacts of everyday life, when we most conspicuously manifest Him to men.

There is further need to stress here what should be the attitude of the ambassador of Christ, in meeting the changed and changing conditions that affect the conventions and practices of daily living, his loyalty to Christian ideals and his boldness in maintaining them.

What are some of the aspects of these new conditions with which we must reckon, and to which we are bound to address ourselves? Here surely, loyalty to the cause we represent must disclose itself and disclose itself in no uncertain way.

The post-war period has witnessed the unleashing of forces that, unrebuked and unrestrained, must ultimately work our ruin. Liberty has lost its dignity and sense of decency and degenerated into brazen license. Wholesome restraints and time-honored conventions have been abrogated. To "commit the oldest kind of sins the newest kind of ways," is the ruling passion of the hour, for "now a time has come to mock at form." This is disclosed in many and conspicuous ways, from habits of dress to social customs and usages. Parental control, the unbroken unity of the home, have for the while lost their place. Marital ties are so loosely effected that they have become, in too many instances, the legal sanctions for an adulterous union. One in every seven marriages is dissolved and the sanctity of the home is thus imperiled. So-called "good society" winks at indiscretions, and the libertine mingles freely with the chaste and wins the plaudits of a bold adventurer, whose exploits give piquancy and zest to the otherwise colorless inanities of the drawing-room. The youth, reared in such an atmosphere, comes to regard chastity as a cheap and worthless virtue, and gives unbridled rein to his passions. A scandal thus becomes a matter that relieves the tedium of a dull and prosaic existence, and lends freshened interest to the news items of the day. Courtrooms where the most salacious and abandoned recitals of evil living are rehearsed, become as magnets to draw those whose moral obliquity finds satisfaction in that which is corrupt and foul and putrid.

The cynic sees, in all this, the triumph of evil over good, and rejoices in the progressive moral depravity of the race. These conditions are reflected in the habits and customs of the hour. They are not restricted to limited areas, nor confined to an abandoned minority. They invade every domain and know no limitations or bounds. Why should they, when homes of accepted decency and refinement open their gates to the pure and the impure, to things of good report and evil report? How shall youth discriminate, when those of mature years and assumed decency show no judgment or discretion? When the pace is so swift that it undermines the physical, shall we be amazed when the moral discloses weakness and decay?

Agnes Repplier wrote an illuminating article sometime ago, entitled "The Repeal of Reticence," in which she indicated fairly and without exaggeration the greater laxity and looseness that characterize both conversation and social habits to-day. To her view a situation is presented, wherein all wholesome restraints are relaxed; all reserves cast aside, and the doors flung open wide to any theme or subject, however unchaste or vulgar it may be.

This is hardly to be wondered at when much of our literature and drama are freely and flagrantly exploiting the lowest and coarsest in life, garnishing it with the most insidious if fascinating forms of expression. The erotic play that portrays the indecencies of life and that does violence to the most sacred of all human institutions is generously patronized by those who profess refinement and respectability. In the corrupting atmosphere of such scenes as the stage has presented within recent months, can we expect anything other than moral degeneracy in those, young and old alike, that witness them? What do selfish playwrights or producers care what results accrue to their sinister and corrupting dramas when their patronage comes from those who boast decency, refinement and respectability?

If parents have no concern for the things that are pure and honest, and of good report, if they feel no responsibility for guarding their children from the leprous and the unclean, why should *they* care, who profit by their indifference?

Can a brief weekly hour of worship cleanse hearts and minds that have been filled for six days with the unwholesome and the unclean? Can any religion, Christian or other, have any appeal for those who have responded readily to the call of the world, the flesh and the devil? There can be no Sunday for such, no day of hallowed associations, with reverence and worship and soul culture. One wonders if we have fallen upon a time when the Church has no message, no voice that will be heard! Yes, one wonders at its silence and indifference, and now and again is amazed at its acceptance of a situation it seems either powerless or unwilling to boldly attack. As guardian of that which is finest and noblest, what a field for him who believes in loyalty to loyalty is presented to-day! The Gospel for an age of sin is too little heard, and the insistent demands of Him who cleansed the Temple precincts with knotted whip-cords are pressed with restraint and caution.

Is it any wonder that our Christian religion loses its appeal to the youth, where its disciplines are relaxed or wholly disregarded by those who profess it? Matthew Arnold declared conduct to be three-fourths of life. Are we addressing ourselves to the remaining fourth, leaving conduct untouched by the high claims of Christ?

You and I believe that Christ came to earth for the enriching and ennobling of men, the cleansing of society, the stabilizing of the home, the making more wholesome and helpful the conditions of life; yes, that it was an abundant life He designed for His children. Are we approximating these demands to-day? And if not, what is to be the future for our children and children's children?

Savonarola dared to attack the flagrant vices of his time, even though they met with royal favor. Courageously he stood against the powerful and reigning houses of his generation, and though they ultimately destroyed his body, his mighty soul has prevailed, and his life is one of the beacons that still lights the world on to better days.

Studdert Kennedy well says that the one thing he is afraid of is "not hell, but life without God, life without anything real to live for." He suggests that which is the vital matter in this critical hour. Can the world go on, except to moral bankruptcy and utter ruin, without the consciousness of God? Will wealth, or power or the genius of man, deliver us from the curse of a Godless world? The tragedy of our present situation is the restlessness and dissatisfaction that prevail. Says Arthur Hoyt: "Our age has three characteristics, easily discerned; an abounding interest in this world, social unrest, and a critical spirit."

Beneath and behind all the swift and highly colored occupations and movements of the hour, reside unrest, dissatisfaction and a longing for something the world cannot give. Well did a Jewish rabbi observe: "A world without order, the product of chance, mechanistically put together and materialistically conceived, a world without moral and spiritual significance, becomes a chaos and a jungle."

The cisterns which men have dug will not and cannot satisfy the thirst of the soul. Man must turn from the uncompensating and unsatisfying to that which gives him peace. Must we not believe that there is weakness somewhere in the Church, yes, conspicuous weakness, that no adequate resistance has been offered to stem the tendencies and violent currents of the hour? The great prophets of other times dared to proclaim a Gospel that demanded heroic service. They were loyal to their Christian convictions. Are we, the later prophets, sufficiently loyal to our standards, to dare to challenge the emboldened forces, that would make havoc of our Christian institutions?

When we come to study fairly and without bias the attitude of the Church, what do we find? Among other things we discover the loss of definiteness of teaching, issuing in relaxed ideals. For a generation the Church has been in the process of retreating and receding from one position to another, until it is difficult to know what its reasonable and sound and logical stand is on any question affecting conduct and belief. A spirit of compromise has seemed to seize it. This with individualistic conceits and consequent loss of authority has so diluted its message that the people themselves are confused and bewildered. Accommodation to local conditions and a conveniently flexible standard, easily adapted to varying needs, have characterized much of its ministry.

Once we frowned on indulgences, too often they are freely granted to-day, and from unworthy motives. The practice of religion has been made so easy, and its word of authority so colorless, that to the reflective it makes little or no appeal. We have largely substituted systems and forms and organizations for deep-seated life controlling religious convictions. A so-called "comfortable Gospel" is out of consonance with that given to men by Jesus Christ.

An anæmic gospel that lays no claim upon discipline makes no appeal to strong, virile men and women. We shall hardly challenge the awakened and self-reliant youth of our time, by presenting to him an easy way of salvation.

Lowered standards and a loose code of ethics substituted for the disciplines imposed by Christ, have lost the Church a large following among the youth, and impaired its influence with men and women of strong convictions. Let us be admonished by the ancient word: "If the trumpet give forth an uncertain sound, who shall prepare himself to the battle?"

You and I believe that Jesus Christ is the supreme need of the hour; that without Him, civilization with all its accumulated treasures is jeopardized. We believe that His teachings, unobscured and undiluted, we are solemnly bound to present to men, whether they like them or not.

The demand for more and better preaching, for more courageous preaching, is urgently recognized. It has lost none of its power, and where it is exercised, men heed it. It is a first-century gospel adapted to twentieth-century needs, and interpreted in twentieth-century language that is demanded. The Archbishop of Canterbury has, in a memorable utterance, set this before the clergy of the English Church, and even the gloomy Dean of St. Paul's makes bold to say that, even if the golden age of preaching *is* past, there is an insistent demand for the informed, courageous and inspired prophet to-day.

Time was when such a condition as I have briefly sketched did not prevail. Time was, when the power of the Church to fix moral standards and to enforce them exceeded even that of the State. Possibly this power was too autocratic and the decrees pronounced too dogmatic. We certainly hold no brief for a ministry that knows no reasonable limitations, and that intrudes itself upon every domain of action. We have separated the things of Church and State and their spheres of service are clearly defined. Let us hope that we have not surrendered the Church's right to declare, and if possible, enforce, its judgment concerning moral standards.

I am addressing this word to men who are to go forth to be opinion-makers, shapers and molders of the moral character of the age in which they live. To aspire to be anything less, is to fail to realize the ideal of this privileged office. It took courage in John Knox to inveigh against the licentious practices of a royal court, but his boldness was felt and his fiery utterances have done much to give moral tone and character to a people of strong will and remarkable tenacity of purpose. Fearlessness in standing for what we hold to be the only wholesome and reasonable course of Christian action may bring us embarrassment, inconvenience and possibly sacrifice. If men in public life will now and again defy even the political machine that gives them preferment, in the interests of consistency and for high moral reasons, surely the advocate of Christ can hardly afford to do less.

Standing almost alone and against the expressed judgment of the leaders of his party for a cause that burned in his soul, a distinguished president of the republic dared to affirm and reaffirm his conviction with these memorable words: "I would rather go down to defeat to-day for a cause that will ultimately triumph, than triumph to-day in a cause that will ultimately know defeat." Brave words these, but made more conspicuously so by the giving of his life for the principle he had enunciated. There is a moral grandeur about the man who believes so strongly in the thing he espouses, that he will give his all in its defense.

Said a great premier of the British empire as the jeers of his colleagues drowned his early utterances: "You will not hear me now, but the time will come when you will hear me;" and it did. Nothing is more remarkable than the prevailing influence of one whose loyalty to a deep conviction or high ideal persists, in spite of all opposition.

That the man with an idea has repeatedly changed the face of things, is writ large on the page of history. The opportunist who would trim his sails to suit every new expression of opinion, who for an hour of praise or popularity will accommodate his utterance or practice to the capricious and fickle wills of those whose favor he seeks, will come at length to know the emptiness and shallowness of such favor. The cheapest of all rewards is that which comes to him who sacrifices ideals and his pledged obligation for the ephemeral praise of men. Cardinal Woolsey to gain the favor of a king lowered his standards, became servile and accommodating to the royal will, and in the end forfeited both favor and his place of eminence and distinction.

Better and nobler the career of the great French preacher, Massilon, whose utterances were so forceful and courageous that they compelled the proud monarch to whom he preached to exclaim, "When I hear other men I am pleased with them, but when I hear you I am displeased with myself." To be "loyal to the royal" in ourselves has compensations that are of greater worth and value than all the gifts and praise of men. To go down to our house justified, with the assurance that we have stood our ground and maintained our cause at all hazards, means to enjoy tranquillity of mind and the approval of Him who was despised and rejected of men.

> You can take your choice [says Dr. Fosdick], you can, if you choose, regard your life as an instant in what Balfour called a brief and discreditable episode. Or you can think of yourself as Jesus Christ thought of himself, as a son of God and heir of all eternity. But don't imagine that it makes no difference how and what you think. It is not chance that the great men of the world have been believing men. They were great men because they had the courage and imagination to believe greatly."

You and I will experience periods when life itself will look dark and shadowy, and the things we stand for seem unappealing and unpopular, but we shall not for an instant strike our colors, or accept the terms of a truce. We are committed to Him, His cause is ours to defend. We have accepted our commission, we will be loyal to Him and His church, for we believe that His cause must ultimately prevail, and that He must come to reign in the hearts of men.

Those who, in the long story of human achievement, rise high above their less aspiring and less courageous fellows, may have known little in life of the favor and praise of their generation. They were too far removed from those who attempted little and gave less, but succeeding ages have rightly appraised their worth and given them their just and enduring meed of distinction. Said a great Archbishop, "There is a loneliness about the life of one who seeks to lead his fellows; the heights to which an exalted office beckons a man, compel him to find his satisfactions within the sanctuary of his own soul." Yes, but within the sanctuary of the soul there may be the deep consciousness of oneness with the high will and purpose of the Eternal Father.

After all's said and done, the disciple may be able to say with his Master, "I have meat to eat, that ye know not of." Victor Hugo's word has a deep significance: "Every man has in him his Patmos, his sphere of larger vision, he is free to go or not go along that frightful promontory of thought, from whose summits the depths of darkness are visible." "Loyalty to Loyalty," is the price of disciplehood.

Rise up, O men of God!
Have done with lesser things,
Give heart and soul, and mind, and strength
To serve the King of Kings.

Rise up, O men of God!
His kingdom tarries long,
Bring in the day of brotherhood
And end the night of wrong.

Lift high the cross of Christ!
Tread where His feet have trod.
As brothers of the Son of man,
Rise up, O men of God!

CHAPTER VI

HIS TECHNIQUE

A large factor that mightily influences our ministry is what we might properly call its technique, which comprises the method, form and conduct of our work. We can readily conceive of one as fully conscious of his authority, fit and equipped for his task, but lacking in efficient service because of a poor technique. While we largely apply this term to the artist and the musician, it certainly has like application to the ministry. It is frequently true that a man has technique, but little else. Grove in his studies in music maintains that "a player may be perfect in technique, and yet have neither soul nor intelligence." All of us have seen this type in the ministry. We are not thinking of technique as a cold, mechanically faultless system by which, with mathematical accuracy, everything we do is carefully weighed and calculated; rather are we thinking of it as the expression of our ministry in terms of order, beauty and power.

There are those rare geniuses who seem to have no precise method or form by which they do their work, they are not amenable to any prescribed method, and they abjure allegiance to all systems. We cannot prescribe for such, and if we did, they would not heed us. We rejoice in their originality, and we admire and reverence their unclassified gifts and powers. The vast majority of us, however, require direction; we cannot build without plans and specifications.

The technique we employ is related to every aspect of our ministry. It discloses itself in the worship we conduct, the sermons we preach, the parochial methods we employ, indeed, it covers the whole range of our activities. To be unmindful and unresponsive to it renders us crude, and our best efforts vain and fruitless.

That there is such a thing as artistry in this sacred office is demonstrably true. It differentiates the work of the skillful from the unskillful, the true fisher of men from him whose unregulated and amateurish endeavors are productive of little or nothing of value. That men will differ in respect to this is evident, but at least they can give themselves more completely to the cultivation of it. Our reading habit, our devotional practices, our preparation for worship and preaching, our pastoral work, yes, our activities in the world, are rendered profitable and effective by the technique that regulates, directs and standardizes all our service.

The need for this precision, orderliness, imagination, spiritual idealism, is one that this present age, possibly more than any other, definitely demands. If the writer, the artist, the musician, the professional man, or indeed the man of affairs, measures his efficiency and his success by this standard, surely we who deal in the things of the spirit, the deepest and holiest things of life, must be diligent in cultivating it. Here let us say with assurance that technique is largely a matter of cultivation, yes, assiduous, unfailing cultivation. We do not come to it at a bound, it is not like some elusive muse that visits us in hours of mental exaltation.

We have throughout these lectures chosen as the fine analogy of our office that of the ambassador. We have attempted to discover the essentials as well as the excellencies that make this office both attractive and efficient. It would not be difficult to prove that, dowered with large gifts and qualities of mind and heart, with a high conception of the privileges and obligations which are implicit in the office itself, our measure of success will be very largely determined by the technique we employ. We have known men of unchallenged intellectual gifts, and indeed of undisputed ability, to signally fail, simply because they lacked an orderly and well-conceived system and plan in the prosecution of their large tasks. Over-assurance or self-confidence, unresponsiveness to what we call the niceties, the refinements of professional service, in their case issued in disappointment and failure. Some one wisely observed that "we cannot rise above the adequacy of the terms we employ."

Technique has to do, let us repeat, with the whole range of our activities. It compels us to give as painstaking care to both big and little tasks as the pianist gives to running the scales, or to rendering with meticulous care a Bach fugue or a Beethoven sonata. Practice, in our office, as in other occupations, makes perfect. How many religious services do we participate in that seem to have every element but this one of careful design and orderly plan; how many sermons do we hear that are void of any seeming purpose or objective?

Dean Sperry speaks of corporate worship as "an artistic recapitulation of Christian experience." He might have included the sermon in this definition. An "artistic recapitulation of Christian experience," does not grow out of some unregulated, uncontrolled impulse, born in a propitious moment of time; it is the resultant of long days of careful preparation, of spiritual enrichment, of soul culture, and of the open window toward Jerusalem.

There doubtless come to one and all of us hours when the inflooding of the soul forces from our lips a message that is born as out of due time. Such a message must not be withheld, it is the sudden flowering of some rich seed of truth that has long lain dormant; but it is a perilous thing to believe that these hours of spiritual illumination are the common experience of the prophet of God. A purely extemporaneous utterance is, in the main, the betrayal of a great and solemn trust. We cannot conceive of the Ambassador's meeting the varying tempers and dispositions and needs of those with whom he has to do, without the most exacting and painstaking preparation.

All this would seem so obvious as to need no word of caution here, but surely the most cursory and superficial study and observation of modern church methods and modern preaching warrants us in emphasizing it anew.

That you and I in the course of our experience will develop a technique largely our own and adapted to certain peculiar conditions, is quite true, and it may be wholly desirable; but let us be sure it is not slovenly and unregulated, rather one that is based upon careful study of the needs of those to whom we minister, and that at all times has design and purpose.

I doubt not that Hadley of Bowery fame became skilled in the art of appealing to and reclaiming the refugees that flocked to his mission, even as Beecher and Jowett, Brooks and Abbott developed for different types of men and women a technique that made them masters of assemblies. Before we dare to approach our large tasks we must determine what our aim and purpose is and the ends we seek to serve. We may not shoot our arrows in the air, nor may we regard an act of worship, private or corporate, as the indulgence of an æsthetic impulse. Those engaged in other offices and occupations may regard the element of chance or good fortune as playing a large part in their success, not so the minister of Christ.

Whether we regard liturgical forms as having value or not, this at least may be said, namely, that these ancient treasuries of devotion do have design and purpose, they stand for a technique in the high art of corporate worship and they guarantee order and decency when reverently used. These venerable formularies were not thrown hastily together, they were fitted part to part like some exquisite mosaic, and when all's said and done, they do insure to the devout worshiper freedom from the eccentricities and idiosyncrasies of the leader of worship. In fine, they recognize and exemplify a technique that contemplates and conserves dignity, precision and reverence. "Decently and in order" is their supreme maxim.

Without seeking to unduly stress this contention we find ourselves justified by a further excerpt from Dean

Sperry's admirable book, *Reality in Worship.* After urging and insisting upon more dignity and precision in the conduct of public worship he says:

> The present chaotic condition of worship in the non-liturgical churches, holds out little hope of any solution of the problem, even by the merest random accident of the laws of chance. The average minister, beyond picking a scripture lesson and hymn to anticipate his sermon, and another hymn to follow the sermon, probably does not give five minutes thought a week to the rest of the service, and has no definite theory as to what is supposed to be happening and what he is theoretically doing, in conducting public worship. Vitality is essential and the service must be grown.

The further word that "the worship of God is an adventure of the Spirit, a flight after the unattainable," needs to be remembered.

Our whole course in these matters is determined by the estimate we place upon worship and its purpose, and the value we put upon preaching and its design. If we are set as leaders to actually lift the spirit of devotion to the highest levels of pure worship, if we are set as prophets to declare to men the whole Gospel of Christ, then surely we must unfailingly cultivate and practice the high art of worship and preaching. That it is an art, and a very great one, is obviously true. It was said of Lafcadio Hearn that "he had the art of jeweling dull phrases"; would that we might assiduously cultivate it.

Men of stammering tongues and mediocre gifts have frequently acquired this art through long and painstaking study; and not infrequently men of eloquent tongue and superior mental qualities have signally failed to gain it because of an improper understanding and appreciation of the ministry's true function and purpose.

Mr. Moody may have lacked a certain refinement of expression that comes from long and exacting academic training, but that he was a master of assemblies and an artist of high rank in the conduct of corporate worship and in the preaching of the Word, was gratefully acknowledged by the multitudes who gladly heard him. His technique may have differentiated him from the preachers of his age, but none will deny him a conspicuous and commanding place among the great apostles of the Church. Shakespeare's words might be applied to such a prophet: "His form and cause conjoined, preaching to stones, would make them capable."

A word of encouragement must be spoken to those who with modesty contemplate the insufficiency of their gifts to meet the demands of the modern church. Great as these demands are, remember always that the persistent cultivation of the spiritual life, the unfailing practice of the devotional habit, coupled with complete consecration, inevitably bring their compensations.

Observation covering a wide field has led us to the inevitable conviction that God uses in a large way the gifts of those who persistently cultivate such talents as He has given them. In obscure places we have repeatedly discovered men of this sort, ministering with rare devotion and skill to the souls committed to their charge. They had developed a technique all their own, and one that was finely adapted to the conditions, they sought to serve. If they ministered to an agricultural community they employed methods designed for that situation; if in a place where artisans, men of toil, were their constituents, they skillfully planned their worship and message to serve the needs of that situation. Both technique and method must adapt themselves to the peculiar needs of those to whom we minister.

We do not for a moment hold that there is a gospel for the rich and another gospel for the poor, we do affirm that the form of its expression must recognize conditions and circumstances that are too evident to be ignored. There are places where the refinements of liturgical forms do not fit. Says the Great Apostle: "There are, it may be, so many kinds of voices in the world, and none of them is without signification." He deprecates speaking in an "unknown tongue" and adds, "I had rather speak five words with my understanding, that by my voice I might teach others, than ten thousand words in an unknown tongue." So great was his capacity to adapt himself to the needs of those to whom he ministered, that he declared himself a Greek to the Greeks, a Jew to the Jews, and a barbarian to the barbarians. He was made all things to all men that by all means he might save some. Here is a standard of excellence in the ministry, worthy of emulation.

We have to-day in the Church men of splendid gifts

who are misfits in the field of their occupation. The technique they employ is utterly unadapted to the needs of those to whom they minister. If a selective method could only be employed in fitting men to fields in which their gifts and talents would have their widest use, we should see the Church's power and influence vastly increased, but probably this will be regarded as a counsel of perfection. One thing at least you and I may avoid, namely, getting into situations for which we have no genius or adaptability.

We recall the ministry of a man of excelling gifts who, in the community he served, exercised a most beneficent influence, but who through restlessness or a desire for change, sought the more colorful life of a great metropolis, only to discover, when it was too late, that he was wholly unadapted to his new environment. His promising and brilliant career came ultimately to tragic disappointment and failure. Blessed is the man who knoweth his limitations. Too great versatility has ruined many a career.

To come to closer range with our problem as it concerns the large interests of our profession, to set before ourselves certain definite ideas or ideals that long experience has demonstrated to be fundamental to efficient service, let us consider what are its indispensable requisites. Out of what does our technique and method spring? What are the dynamics of a ministry of real power? Are there well-prescribed standards of practice that the ministry must recognize and follow?

The threefold aspects of our office, namely, those of prophet, priest and pastor, are vitally related, and must always be so considered. To think of them as separate and unrelated offices, means to lose their cumulative value. To consider them as interrelated parts of a well-ordered, well-rounded ministry, means to guarantee to our office the highest efficiency and the most satisfying results.

Someone has well said that "the day takes its shape from the morning"; in a word, we discover and determine our objective and our capacity to achieve what we seek when we begin by recognizing the value of an ordered and well-planned life. "What we are comes before what we do."

With this conviction, we cannot too strongly urge the importance of everything antecedent to the spoken word; for its power, its adaptability, its compelling and convincing appeal spring inevitably out of what has come to us out of our daily study and experience. The message of value must be the expression of our own deep and unfailing conviction. It cannot be the expression of what someone else has felt or experienced; it must be our own. Other men's sermons may be altogether appealing, but they are appealing because the men who uttered them had *lived* them; they were the articulate expression of their own experience.

As a striking illustration of this, we learned more of the real soul of Dean Inge in the smallest and least scholarly of his manifold writings in a little book he wrote that was inspired by the life and death of his little daughter, than we did in all his highly polished and finished essays. In this, the least pretentious of his writings, the heart and soul of the man find their truest and noblest expression. To attempt to reproduce such a message without such a background of experience, is the part of folly. Fundamentally and essentially, our message, however simple its form, must be the product of our own thought, enforced by our own experience.

We recall in this connection an episode related to us by the late Bishop Greer, who was himself a preacher of rare gifts. Let me quote his own statement: "One evening, after a taxing day that had been fully occupied with manifold parochial duties, I strolled over to my parish house in East Forty-second Street to see what activities were in progress. On entering, I found that a religious meeting was being held in one of the large rooms. It was a characteristic East Side crowd made up of many types. I had seated myself in an obscure place in the back of the room, when presently a rather elderly woman, shabbily dressed with a faded gray shawl about her head, arose and spoke. I soon found myself deeply absorbed in what she was saying. In a modest, simple, but singularly impressive way, she was relating her religious experience. As her story progressed, I found myself profoundly moved by its recital. Pathos, deep spiritual conviction characterized her every word. When she concluded her utterance, I was so deeply moved that I quietly withdrew, and as I wended my way homeward, I could not lose the spell that her homely, deeply impressive utterance had made upon me." With a touch of fire in his voice he added: "That was a real message, born out of a great spiritual experience, it was the kind of message that counts."

The humble woman in an East Side mission had

taught the eloquent rector of St. Bartholomew's one of the most vital lessons of the prophetic ministry. "It was the kind of message that counts." The woman with the faded gray shawl had told that of which she had knowledge.

May we not say that this is the most indispensable element in any message that has vital power. That the listener is conscious of this, yes, and that it constitutes the chief appeal in any sermon, is demonstrably true. Even the form which our pulpit ministry takes is subordinate to it. "Ye are my witnesses," said Christ, and to be a witness whose testimony has convincing power, we must speak that which we know, that which we have actually experienced. "I know whom I have believed," said the great preacher and apostle; little wonder that he moved whole cities and converted multitudes.

If there is one weakness in modern preaching more conspicuous than another, it is the lack of this element of testimony born out of experience. We cannot convince the jury before whom we plead, unless we can compel them to believe, that what we say, we know to be true. As Dr. Hocking expressed it: "A religion that a man does not know he has, is of no importance."

Obviously, maturity brings with it richer and deeper experiences that serve to make our messages more compelling and varied; but while this is true, it is interesting to note that some of the sermons preached by the greatest of prophets were delivered in the early days of their service. It was then, with a freshness of conviction and an enthusiasm for what they held, that they gave forth their most compelling messages. That our wider reading and broader experience do affect our utterances, is indisputably true; nevertheless, the flaming zeal that comes with the deep convictions of our earlier ministry mightily influences those to whom we bear our messages. It would be a difficult thing to determine just when our pulpit power is at its best.

We have known men whose maturer, riper scholarship tended to make them less effective in their pulpit work. This furnishes no plea for an uninformed and ignorant ministry; it is simply an observation that is too frequently true. There may be so much of the purely intellectual in our message that the very refinement of its expression may render it unappealing and unconvincing. You recall what Mr. Moody once said: "What's the use of talking to these people about two Isaiahs, when the great majority do not know that there is one."

The greatest teacher I ever had was one of the poorest of preachers. His forte was to teach others how and what to preach, and in this he rendered a great service; but his students could never seem to forget that, compelling as he was in the classroom, he could not exemplify his theories in the pulpit. Protracted study had taken from him certain qualities that are indispensable to effective preaching.

Your business and mine is to so develop and stir our latent powers and to so prove by test and trial our religious conviction that we shall come to our people week by week with a message that is the recital of our own deep experience. We may not be gifted, our speech may not be touched with eloquence, it will, nevertheless, not be lacking in enkindling, converting power, because it has the unmistakable hallmark of our own life's experience upon it.

I like that brief word written concerning the Forerunner: "John did no miracle, but all that he spake of this man was true." There was nothing of wizardry about him, none of the gifts that others had did he covet, he was simply the "voice of one," but so compelling was he that multitudes thronged forth from Jerusalem's streets to hear him.

There is nothing unique about our present age, so far as the popularity of preaching is concerned. The people of New York and Boston and Chicago, yes, and the people of the quiet hamlets and villages are as responsive to the real message of a real man as they ever were, but reality is the sine qua non of fitness in both the man and his message. There is much cheap talk being heard about the lost power of the pulpit; it is directed largely at a kind of pulpit message that itself is cheap, unworthy and unwholesome. We cannot but believe that valid criticism of much of our present-day preaching is based upon the hearing of themes that are unworthy to be characterized as pulpit messages. The lowering of the high standards of the pulpit by the introduction of themes and subjects that have neither cultural nor spiritual value, too often brings our office into disrepute and contempt. The appeal of the central truths of the Gospel teachings of Jesus, these have never lost their charm or their persuasive power.

A recent critic of the modern pulpit makes the searching inquiry: "Shall we send our children to Church?" He follows his query with the statement,

"The fundamental appeal of Christianity is as a way of life. It is the spiritual interpretation of the universe in the light of a great personality. The perpetual freshness and vitality of its appeal have survived the incrustation of creeds and dogmas that men have erected about it." He concludes his query with a further observation: "Whether Protestantism can so interpret the life and work of Jesus of Nazareth as to restore the radiance of a personality that it is not hard to think of as potent to transform and save the world—this is the momentous question that our churches have at their door." This earnest seeker after a more appealing ministry, especially as it relates to the youth, emphasizes the supreme need for a fresh and continued emphasis upon the "radiant personality," that constitutes the Church's only claim to continuing favor and the only source of its increasing power.

On every hand we hear this appeal; every age repeats it, its volume grows as the years multiply. Where it has been heeded, the Church has waxed strong and persuasive. Where it has been ignored, the Church has forfeited the confidence of men and the fires on its altar have burned low. What of our message to-day?

What is the dominant note in twentieth-century preaching? As ambassadors how do we meet the needs of a situation that at best is fraught with perils that at times threaten the security and stability of the Church as an institution? If we rightly sense the mind of our time, it is expressing in no uncertain terms what it demands of the Church. Crowds of eager listeners throng the temple where the radiant personality is the central theme. Crowds, reverent crowds bow low, where seemly worship is coupled with a seemly and reverent message. No matter what we as preachers or messengers may think of worship and sermon, the world at large is appraising what we purvey, and it will either gladly accept or as readily reject our offering.

Time was, when an autocratic church could, in its council chambers, determine what it would give and what it would withhold. Not so to-day. "A voice from the crowd" in the person of a great layman, speaking from this lecture platform, sets forth in clear and unmistakable but respectful terms, what the crowd thinks and demands. Shall the voice be heeded?

Obviously, we will not, nor can we compromise our position as guardians of the oracles, or conservers of the Church's sacraments, nor is this demanded. We shall not close our eyes nor deaden our ears to new manifestations of truth, nor need we; but if we are quick to understand our age we shall speedily give the altar and the pulpit their rightful place, and make both serve the high ends of a true and reverent worship and spiritual culture. Too much cannot be said respecting these things. An over-magnified message and an ill-considered form of worship cannot be made to serve the needs in the case. The two are vitally related, they are designed to serve one purpose and one purpose only, namely, the spiritual enrichment of those to whom we minister.

Said one of our foremost professors of homiletics: "I regard the preparation for reverent worship as transcending in importance even the preparation we make for our pulpit ministry. As a matter of fact, the latter is largely conditioned by the former." We do not believe anything we may say concerning the technique of the message will be of value, unless we can identify it with the holy office of worship. Consistency here is indispensable to an effective ministry.

Mr. Beecher's prayers constitute a liturgy in themselves; they show more meticulous care than even his glowing messages; indeed, they were the inspiration that to preacher and people alike made the messages move with power and unction. No matter what we may say concerning our modern pulpit work, we dare not be boastful when we consider much that characterizes the conduct of modern worship.

What has all this consideration of the things of worship to do with the prophet's message, its form and substance? Everything. The worship is the background, the setting if you will, of the message. If the message is jewel-like, its beauty and its charm will be largely determined by the kind of setting we give it. After all, we preach for the profit and edification of those to whom we minister, and what we do before we preach mightily affects the receptivity of those to whom we preach.

In this whole matter of the relation of worship to preaching we may not forget the place which music holds in the ordering of corporate service. To again quote Mr. Beecher, "Music is one of the most important auxiliaries of the preacher." How frequently, through misdirected zeal this auxiliary fails! And why? Largely because in our conception of our office we give no heed to its place and importance.

I would not undertake to preach a sermon or conduct a service as a pastor without determining beforehand the hymns and frequently the anthems to be sung. A service should be symphonic in character, and music is one of its primary elements. A secularized organist and a secularized choir, wholly out of sympathy with the spiritual implications of the ministry of music, impair if they do not destroy the reverence and dignity of corporate worship. Here I would make the leader of worship, the messenger in the pulpit, an autocrat.

Music compels the members of a congregation to coalesce. As a unifying power, rightly and reverently used, it is quite incomparable. Some choirs and some choir-masters are the enemies of both preacher and congregation, and neither worship nor message can survive their baleful influence.

That more consideration must be given by the pastor to the precision and order of corporate worship in all its parts and details is urgently needed. Situations frequently arise where, without careful direction and autocratic control, the musical portions of the service become a distinct hindrance to decent and orderly worship, and an embarrassment to preacher and people. To refer again to Mr. Beecher, he says concerning organists and organs that he "cares not if the player be a Beethoven and the organ the most magnificent that ever was constructed, they are both servants, and their glory is subordination." He is surely right in this, and it needs vigorous insistence in most of our churches.

I shall be remiss if I do not here urge the vital importance of making all church music conserve the deep things of worship. Here again it is a question of technique, the utter adaptation and refinement of music to the ends of spiritual culture. Just now in this age of Jazz, where discord has displaced harmony, an appeal needs to be made for the restoration of the "concord of sweet sound." You and I may not be experts in music, but we certainly ought to know what helps and what hinders the devotional spirit. To conserve the eternal fitness of things is no small part of our task.

Where a service is non-liturgical, the most meticulous care is demanded to render it harmonious. Scripture lessons, hymns, anthems, prayers and sermon, are all essentially related parts of what should be a symmetrical and harmonious whole. The Psalms of Degrees illustrate what we have in mind. Orderly sequence, with a rising crescendo, and above all else, definiteness and fixity of purpose, these are imperatively demanded.

Primarily we are leaders of worship. We shall not be heard for our much speaking, and again we need to be reminded of the folly of vain repetitions. The art of prayer is a very great one, and nothing requires more refinement of expression or more delicacy of feeling.

We attended the funeral recently of a distinguished presbyter, where the prayer and the address differed from one another only in this, that one was a eulogy of the person deceased addressed to God, and the other a eulogy of our brother addressed to the congregation. Here was a startling demonstration, not by any means uncommon, of a misconception of the design and purpose of prayer. I need only add that the eulogies in both instances were admirable.

You recall that Professor Royce speaks of the Church as a "Community of Memory and Hope." Would that we might always remember this in the conduct of its services. To stir the depths of memory until the choice gifts of God are gratefully acknowledged, to inspire hope until the soul is rejuvenated and renewed through freshened contact with the God of hope, surely this is our high and holy privilege. We can make no better resolve to govern us in these matters than that of the Apostle: "I will pray with the spirit, and I will pray with the understanding also."

In all that we have said thus far, we have not undervalued or subordinated the importance of the sermon, we can only see the sermon in the relation it bears to the whole act of worship itself. We repeat, what goes before it largely determines its value and power.

What of its technique? What of its form? If we shall take as the supreme model that of our Lord's great sermon, it will be winsome with the compulsions of an irresistible love. "He knew what was in man," and knowing this He knew the power of the love motive. There is little or nothing of argument in any of His utterances. His chief endeavor was to reveal to men their truer and better natures. Only once were His words spoken with vehemence, and then only when

He sought to strip away the coverings of a superficial and purely external semblance of religion. "Woe unto you, Scribes and Pharisees, hypocrites, for ye make clean the outside of the cup and of the platter, but within they are full of extortion and excess." To every type save this, tenderness, solicitude for the forgotten, better self, characterized His message. Repellent as sin was, He banished it with the word, "Neither do I condemn thee, go and sin no more." He encouraged a languishing faith by disclosing its latent power and beauty. He so exalted the deep values of life that men everywhere caught a new sense of its possibilities and of its real purpose.

So profoundly convinced of the supreme value of His method was Frederick Robertson, England's peerless preacher, that he wrote in the preface of his volume of sermons:

> I may be wrong in my opinion, but it is one of deep conviction, gained long ago, that no amount of external evidence in the way of proof of the truth of Christianity, is worth anything in the way of saving a human soul. I think a bold, faithful, experimental preaching rarely fails to hit the mark.

We do not convert men through long and laborious argument. We do compel them by holding before them the irresistible claims of Jesus.

To approach a congregation with the idea that they are unresponsive to the appeal of the Gospel, means to forfeit their interest and glad response. We recall those splendid words of St. Paul, "The law made nothing perfect, but the bringing in of a better hope did."

Evelyn Underhill truly says:

> Human religion is simply a live wire, along which the energy of charity comes to man's soul from the Eternal, and returns again to its source. Thus, the doctrine or practice which does not convey charity ceases to be religious; whilst the most extreme sacramental act, the simplest and least articulated aspiration, insofar as these mediate the Eternal, truly minister to the spiritual life of men. Religion in all its depth and range, its wide and lovely variousness, witnesses to this truth, assuring us that it is the strange privilege of men to ascend, by means not only of thought but of things, by symbol and by act, to that which transcends all thoughts and all things.

Your ministry and mine must be a healing ministry. It must reveal to men life's unfulfilled possibilities. "Man is not so much a fact as a possibility," some one observes. We deal with patients who are sick, and we must minister to their needs; how shall we do it effectively unless we employ methods that are in consonance with His methods? "The Gospel for an age of sin," this surely, but a Gospel of hope that compels by the persuasions of love.

A stern dogmatism repels, an appeal to all that is best and truest restores. This Gospel of hope is supremely needed to-day. To restore a lost confidence, to disclose, yes, to discover, latent virtues and soul qualities, long forgotten, this is our highest and holiest privilege. To develop in this a technique, a system, a method, requires a deep understanding of the will and purpose of Christ. Ambassadors of the Gospel of hope, what higher distinction may we covet? "The love of Christ constraineth me," wrote the apostle. Surely this was the method of the Christ. Has the Gospel as we preach it to-day lost this love motive? Does our later conception of what constitutes the twentieth-century technique of sermon-making and preaching, rule out that which was the supreme characteristic of Christ's ministry to men?

A critical and severely censorious type of preaching on the one hand, and a luke-warm, colorless preaching on the other, effect little in the way of spiritual culture. Let us beware of that kind of preaching that in an effort after breadth, becomes utterly superficial and unprofitable. We dare not be broader or more tolerant than Christ. Charity that covers a multitude of sins without attempting to eradicate them, is a false kind of charity. Dr. Gordon well said that "it is a matter of history that the broadening of creeds has usually been accompanied by a great decay of zeal on the part of believers." To pare down the eternal truths until they are but shadows, means to render them feeble and impotent.

What of our office as teachers? "As a teaching force, Protestantism has abdicated," says a university president. Commenting on this a recent writer observes: "Question a Roman Catholic concerning his religion, and you get a definite reply. He has been taught. Question a Protestant, and there comes a puzzled look, then an answer so vague that, once he has got his ideas out in front of him, he seems more perplexed than before."

While this observation may be exaggerated in both cases, it is indisputably true that Protestanism, in our generation, has made a sorry mess of its teaching office. The average pastor gives scant heed to his Sunday school, turning it over to the care of untrained and often immature voluntary teachers. While the sermon is supposed to be in the nature of an instructon, in the large majority of cases, it is an exhortation. "Be good and you'll be happy," too frequently characterizes the substance of the pulpit message.

I know of a notable case where in an attempt to make a night service more appealing, the rector introduced a series of systematic Bible instructions, with the result that immediately a congregation of over a thousand was produced and the experiment is going forward with unabated interest. Such a method taxes the preacher, if he purveys the right pabulum more than ordinary preaching, but demonstrates its effectiveness by its results.

What does the average Church member really know concerning the most vital things of the faith? Compared with his knowledge of other subjects, it is negligible.

A man of exceptional intellectual ability observed to me recently that, while he was confirmed at sixteen, he had so little knowledge of the deep meaning of Christ's sacramental system that he had abstained from participating in the Communion service for over thirty years. "I never had adequate instruction at any time in this and in other vital matters that concern the essential doctrines of Christianity," he said. A tragic statement, but one that is altogether too common.

The *ecclesia docens* seems to have lost its place of distinction in our generation. Every kind of propaganda flourishes; the teachers of new and strange doctrines are voluble and persistent, the Christian propagandist alone seems to be inactive. Is the ministry afraid to assume its chief office? Have we lost our zest for meditation and study to such an extent that we are incapable of instructing our people in the unchanging, fundamental principles of the Christian religion?

The incapacity of the youth, in particular, to resist the inroads of certain modern schools of thought, leaves them floundering and helpless; hence, they repeatedly fall the victims of the alluring nostrums of the hour. Certain modern cults have literally builded their institutions upon the poorly laid foundations of the Christian Church.

Ignorance is unquestionably at the root of much of the apostasy and moral dereliction of our age. More education, education based upon accurate knowledge, unbiased and unembarrassed by individualistic conceits, is the greatest need of the Church today.

That there is a body of doctrine, that there is a well-defined system of ethics, yes, a philosophy of life, in the New Testament, is clearly evident. It needs to be taught, and taught systematically, and with a background of knowledge that makes it both fascinating and compelling.

If necessary it were better that we abandoned ourselves to this vitally important matter, rather than through a too-discursive ministry we attempted to carry the burdens of a highly administered but too mechanical organization.

The Man Nobody Knows, from the pen of a journalist, becomes a sensation, because it suggests a situation so common and so widely recognized. The widespread demand for this book illustrates, in a striking way, the need for more definite and specific instruction covering the life and ministry of Jesus. If your office and mine is not a teaching office it is untrue to its highest ideal.

Clever and brilliant preaching may stir the minds and consciences of men to wholesome living, but wholesome living cannot be maintained by sporadic revivals of interest, it proves utterly ephemeral, unless nourished by an intelligent and sustained religious conviction. To give a reason for the hope that is in us, means to be able to resist the sophistries and speculations of the hour.

We who preach must know what we believe and why we believe, else we cannot communicate our convictions to others. The substance of the New Testament we must know, and the best information born of the ripest scholarship must be ours. Theology, once called the "queen of the sciences," has been shorn of her proud distinction, and religious education has largely been given into the hands of sincere but uninformed amateurs in the art of teaching.

If the present situation does not give us deep concern, then it is because we are unwilling to properly evaluate it, or are coldly indifferent to it. God give us teachers, high-souled, consecrated, informed teachers, to save us from an ignorance that threatens our peace and our very security. All this has to do with the technique of our office, indeed, it is indispensable to it.

Plan systematically, for certain seasons each year, courses of sermons. Dare to repeat themes that have to do with spiritual growth and enrichment. Take nothing for granted. The most intelligent in your congregations look to you for instruction in the things of religion.

If you discourse of science, art, literature or economics, you doubtless have in your hearing those better informed than yourself. They will discount your utterances. If you keep to your own special theme, and it is big enough to engage all your gifts, you are on safe ground. The Bible is your textbook, enriched by the Christian experience of the centuries and illuminated by the lives of the saints through many generations. If it does not meet all the needs in the case, then it is because you do not understand it, or you have chosen the wrong profession.

Your age is not asking for a diluted Gospel, but for the truth as it is in Christ Jesus.

Dear brethren, let us not handle the word of God carelessly or deceitfully. Fearlessly and courageously but with unfailing love, let us preach that Gospel that has lost none of its power to ransom men from the thraldom of sin. No refinement of technique may serve as a substitute for a Gospel simply, understandingly, forcibly preached. The ambassador for Christ must present his credentials as one whose messages bear upon them the imprimatur of his Sovereign. The messages are ours because we speak them, they will prove profitable only as men know they proceed from Him.

So order your ministry, in all its parts, pastoral, priestly, prophetic, that you may become an artist—an artist whose soul is aflame with a passion for souls, so shall your holy office come to serve the needs of men, and your life be linked with those who have kept the faith and been found worthy at length to stand before the Son of Man.

CHAPTER VII

HIS PERILS

One of the finest admonitions ever given to a great leader is that directed to Moses at the height of his career. "Be thou for the people to Godward, that thou mayest bring the causes unto God." The incident recorded in the narrative from which this passage is taken has about it a distinctly modern flavor. A great leader had reached an impasse in his work. With fine enthusiasm and a ready desire to serve he had assumed increasingly weighty obligations. Day by day they had grown upon him. He had come to feel not only their burdening weight but their large importance. He had come to regard himself as alone competent to deal with the multifarious problems of the people, who gladly acknowledged his leadership. At length it had become clearly evident that both leader and people, the worker and the work, were suffering serious impairment by reason of the concentration of labor.

At this crisis, one older and wiser thus addressed the leader, "What is this thing that thou doest to the people? Why sittest thou, thyself, alone, and all the people stand by thee from morning until evening?" And Moses said, "Because the people come unto me to inquire of God. When they have a matter they come unto me, and I judge between one and another." And Moses' father-in-law said unto him, "The thing that thou doest is not good, thou wilt surely wear away both thou and this people that is with thee, for this thing is too heavy for thee. Thou art not able to perform it thyself alone." Then followed the high and solemn admonition: "Be thou for the people to Godward, that thou mayest bring the causes unto God."

It was to release the great leader of the people from burdening details, to give him larger freedom for his weightier and more important tasks that the word of solemn warning was given. To place him in his supreme and sovereign place as God's accredited agent, his chosen representative, the plea was made.

I repeat, the situation has about it a suggestive modern flavor. It rehearses very accurately the conditions of life under which the modern priest and prophet of God labors to-day. Professional standards change with changing customs. New conditions compel new methods, and a swiftly moving age demands mental alertness and a speeding up of mechanisms and agencies. The circuit-rider with his quaint saddle-bags, his homely raiment and his itinerant habits, would hardly fit an age that is Mercury footed, that considers space in terms of lightning speed, and employs the ether to transmit its messages to distant and unseen hearers. The day in which we live with its colorful and kaleidoscopic life lays a claim upon the minister that his brother of another generation never knew. The occupations of the modern, busy pastor are so varied and call for gifts and qualities so diverse that neither university nor seminary can adequately equip him to meet the clamorous demands of the present hour. It would hardly be wide of the mark to say that the twentieth-century conception of the ministry calls for a larger variety of gifts and talents than any other calling or profession of which we have knowledge.

Administration, with all that that implies, preaching, pastoral work, a liberal indulgence in secular concerns and social occupations, multitudinous committees, boards and beneficent institutions, these and unnumbered and unnamed agencies lay their pressing claims upon his time, while the ever-pressing demands of a depleted exchequer shadow his path, and make hard and difficult his way. Truly, here is an office that, in our modern conception of it, calls for physical robustness, large and varied mental and spiritual gifts, the cunning of the statesman, coupled with the genius of the economist, the vision of the seer with the hopefulness of the optimist. We would not lessen one whit its greatness, or its broad and genial outlook, but the large question, yes, the compelling question with which we are faced to-day is: "Has this later approximation of ministerial efficiency given it a place of power, compared with which the priests and prophets of another age seem poor and mean?" In fine, has the new norm or standard demonstrated its fitness to serve an age that is distracted and confused? Chesterton said somewhere, "Christianity has not been tried and found wanting. It has been tried and found difficult." He was attempting to answer the oft-repeated challenge that Christianity as a system has signally failed.

We are confronted to-day with conditions within and without the Church that call for the finest and most discriminating judgment and the most statesmanlike and balanced consideration. Without the slightest touch of ungenerous pessimism, we are compelled to deal with a situation that is real and not fancied. We are in a world that, after an awful strain, is seeking to re-adjust itself and to reckon with systems and institutions that have failed it in the time of its Gethsemane. It is not our obligation to deal with economic and financial problems that call for experts, it is our obligation to set our own house in order and to discover, if possible, the weaknesses in our present system.

To many of us it is becoming increasingly evident that there are maladjustments that demand consideration and correction; methods, systems and agencies that need recasting and revision, standards and principles that call for renewed emphasis. Our present system, as it relates to the Church's function in the world, is widely at variance with the standards set by those who gave it its charter and enriched it with a ministry that is the wonder and despair of succeeding ages.

True, the Church must not be static. It must be dynamic and sufficiently flexible to adjust itself to changed and changing conditions. In a modern world it must be modern. It is compelled to reckon with a new order of things in which there is a persistent demand for reconstruction and readaptation to meet new needs. At such a time, to ignore this demand would be the part of folly. While the fundamental things of our faith may not be changed, they may be subject to re-statement and their application made more practical as they bear upon our modern life. There is to-day a widespread yearning for the mighty principles of life given to the world by Jesus Christ. Nothing is more evident than the sovereign and supreme place He occupies in the affections of men.

That the world has turned its vision to Him who spake as never man spake, is demonstrably true. In spite of all discussions and controversies, the regnancy of Christ stands unchallenged and unchallengeable. We are not called upon to consider His place as the "holiest among the holy," nor the incomparable character of His teaching. He needs no apologist. What we are called upon seriously to consider is our own relation to Him as his teachers and exemplars and the adaptability of our methods to make Him sovereign in the hearts of men. In fine, we are compelled to appraise anew the methods and mechanisms we have called into being and their fitness to serve the high purposes of His kingdom.

The most cursory study discloses a condition within the Church's life that should give us pause. Our boasted statistics that disclose growth along certain lines (lines that do not accurately measure spiritual development) furnish no adequate or fair indication as to the vitality and efficiency of the Church as an institution. Neither growth in material things, nor even proportionate increase in numbers, may be taken as evidences of the Church's spiritual vitality. A reappraisal of values, a thorough inventory of assets and liabilities, this alone will serve the purposes of a situation as critical as the present.

With unbiased frankness then, cost what it may,

let us, even though we may be doing it hastily and partially, survey the present situation and our relation to it. To enter, or even to continue in this high profession to-day, without a fair and reasonable knowledge of the value of those agencies and institutions that we have come to regard as normal parts of the Church's enterprise, is not only unwise, but may prove disastrous. It will be readily admitted that large and sweeping changes have come into the life of the Church during the past forty or fifty years. While its forms of worship and sacramental system have remained practically intact, new and later agencies have attached themselves to the Church as an institution, their avowed purpose being to stimulate and promote a declining interest, especially on the part of the youth.

Within the life-time of most of us, a distinctly new instrumentality has been added, known as the "institutional department" of the Church. It began in great centers of population and rapidly spread, until to-day even the small community has its modest equipment designed to meet the social demands of the community in which it is placed. That this new department has played a conspicuous and useful part is clearly evident. Its purpose was to humanize the Church as an institution, to make more clear, particularly to the youth, the high purposes of a Christian faith that sought, in the language of the Master, the "more abundant life." To make a man "every whit whole"; to deal with bodies as well as souls; to effect physical robustness and spiritual vitality, all this was the high aim that lay behind this form of Christian endeavor.

Parish houses under this new system came to be as costly, if not more costly, than church buildings. In some instances they combined not only every form of social, recreational, and physical entertainment, but they also comprehended many other agencies that had to do with human needs. If a careful survey could be made of the spiritual results accruing to these costly enterprises, one wonders what it might disclose. Someone caustically observes that "we have machinery but no motion." Matthew Arnold maintained: "We move men by the spirit we are of, rather than by the machinery we employ."

I recall with great vividness an observation made to me some twenty-five years ago by one of the most brilliant prophets of the Church. He had been studying closely a large and costly enterprise in which I was then engaged and he had reached the conclusion that, while it was exceedingly fascinating as a new and unique venture, it bore no necessary relation to the large spiritual concerns of the Church. I was startled by his observation when he said, "Your great agency is altogether fine and admirably conceived, but I make the prediction that the time will come when, instead of proving a door of access to the Church, it will become an avenue of exit from it."

I am not prepared to admit that his observation was wholly accurate; on the other hand, I am prepared to say that the institutional department of the Christian Church has in no small degree deflected the ministry from its primary purpose, and possibly more than any other single cause we might name, impaired its great functions, commonly designated, pastoral and prophetic, which in another age were its chief adornments and most compelling virtues.

In an age that was characterized by mechanical skill and efficiency, the Church felt the need of newer and more perfect mechanisms for its enterprise. No one doubts the consistency or purity of its motive, nor the desirability of much that it called into being. That institutionalism served, and will continue to serve a large purpose, is generally admitted. It is not against institutionalism as such that we inveigh, it is rather that we call in question its exaggerated importance, and the spiritual results that have accrued to it.

Where any mechanism or agency impairs the major functions of the Church's enterprise, or curtails in any wise the real purpose of the Christian ministry, we are bound to inquire as to its utility and value. The modern complexity and variety of Church administration has brought the ministry itself dangerously near the breaking point. It has laid upon the shoulders of the Church's chosen leaders burdens too heavy to be borne. It has brought about a situation that has resulted in the impairment of the pastoral and prophetic office. It has called for an outlay of time, money and energy, the volume of which has mounted from year to year. It has diverted interest and enthusiasm from religion, and given them to pastimes and recreations. It has put the Church in competition with secular agencies, and placed it at a disadvantage it cannot readily overcome. Most deplorable and tragic of all, it has shifted the emphasis from a concern for souls to a concern for bodies.

That the Church has a definite concern for the

physical and social well-being of men, goes without saying. The question which this modern institutional agency has raised, is largely one of economy and ultimate purpose; economy, as it relates primarily to the distribution of the clergyman's time; purpose, as it relates to the spiritual development of those whom it seeks to serve.

A Church engrossed in the most wholesome and appealing forms of social recreation, essential and valuable as these may be, must ultimately lose much of its influence and power in promoting the spiritual enrichment and elevation of the community in which it is placed.

We register no plea against the social or recreational side of the Church's endeavor. We do maintain that if this phase of its enterprise is to be continued, it must be subordinated to the major things for which the Church itself stands. If it cannot be made a means to the one supreme end of character-building, which we submit is the Church's highest aim and end, it must be regarded as a menace to the Church as an institution.

At the very beginning, the Apostles found themselves confronted with a situation that so seriously impaired their spiritual ministry that they were forced to abandon the routine of their growing administrative obligations, and to secure the services of fit men to put over this business. They conceived that their primary work had to do with things spiritual, the ministry of the Word and prayer. With this lofty vision of their obligation, they set apart others to perform the work of administration. The modern Church is faced with a still more serious situation, and if its higher ministeries are to be maintained, it must follow the practice of the church of an earlier day. In other words, if the Church of our day is to contribute its large share in meeting the needs of our modern, complex life, it must safeguard its ministry from becoming so utterly entangled in administrative and mechanical concerns that its spiritual functions are impaired or rendered inefficient.

For my own part, after over thirty years of extensive and costly indulgence in institutional work, I question very seriously many of the methods it employs. If it cannot be demonstrated that all its enterprise issues in spiritual rejuvenation and enrichment, it has no valid place as part of the Church's program. If it hinders in any degree the largest expression of the Church's vital ministry, it must be regarded as a piece of machinery that has become obsolete and worthless. No word too strong or urgent may be spoken against any enterprise, no matter how attractive or appealing it may be, that retards, rather than accelerates, the spiritual functions of the Church. Let us build the whole man, body, mind and soul, but let us be very sure that it *is* the whole man we are conserving. While we minister to his body, let us not forget his soul.

The progress of the early Church, its amazing conquests and triumphs, constitute the brightest page in its annal. "They went everywhere preaching," is written concerning these peasant evangelists. The priest and the prophet were one, the evangel and the sacraments had their interpreter, theirs was a balanced ministry. Every great spiritual movement that has swept over continents and ushered in great revivals of religion has been characterized by strong preaching. The popularity of the prophet's office has never been challenged. It stands to-day in a more commanding and strategic position than it has ever known.

We dare to say that religion, rightly purveyed, is the most utterly popular theme being presented to-day. So popular indeed is it that it holds the most commanding place in the utterances of our leading statesmen and in the editorials of our secular press. The opportunity before the Church to-day has never been equaled, if with Christian statesmanship and humility it applies itself to its high task. If it will but divorce its ministry from harassing administrative details, if it will but witness with all its prophetic and sacramental power to its supreme business, if it will avoid entangling alliances with institutions that are unrelated to its vast enterprise, in a word, if it will once again make Him alone supreme, it will enter upon the new day of its mightiest conquest.

The age is calling for a crusade and the crusader's spirit. It is calling for a Church for religion only. It has its every need met by multiform and ever-increasing agencies. It seeks its house of worship for spiritual refreshment and renewal. The multitude is at our gates to-day, saying: "Sirs, we would see Jesus." Woe be to us if we obscure the world's vision of Him, or fail with blood earnestness to preach His saving gospel.

Only recently Dean Inge, surveying the present situation in the hope of seeing signs of an approaching religious revival, said:

> No signs of such a spiritual revival are fairly traceable in the chaos and babel that war has left behind. We see not our tokens, there is not one prophet more. Perhaps he is among us somewhere, unknown. He may be a school-boy or an apprentice. When he comes, I am disposed to think that he will choose to speak to this generation neither from the pulpit, nor from the platform, nor from the printed page, but from the stage. A great dramatist may help us to find our souls.

The Dean of St. Paul's was never more gloomy than in this statement. We cannot hold with him that, apart from the Church's ministry, this revival is to come; but we do hold that it can only come when that ministry is unfettered and unhampered by burdens that to-day restrict and restrain it in its largest service.

President Coolidge, with prophetic voice recently declared as he observed the fatuous endeavors to restore world order and peace through legislative methods that, "we cannot depend upon government to do the work of religion. There is no way by which we can substitute the authority of law for the virtue of man." He was pleading for the restoration of the truest and best in our Christian faith and practice.

I am moved thus to speak, because I apprehend that young men entering the ministry to-day, are drawn with a strange fascination to those mechanical devices that have been called into being in recent years, and that have so completely engrossed the time and service of the Christian ministry. It is always easier to adapt oneself to what one finds in the way of means and agencies than it is to blaze a new trail or to discover new ways of doing the Church's work. It is ever popular to follow the line of least resistance. The Christian ministry will speedily degenerate and lose its place of power if it continues to exalt machinery.

A passion for organization has literally seized the mind of the Church. An inordinate desire to multiply agencies and mechanisms threatens to destroy the higher functions of the Christian ministry. Says a modern close observer of the Church and her ways:

> There never was a time when the Church was as busily engaged in such a multitude of outward tasks, and hardly a time when the Church was more inwardly restless, more spiritually dissatisfied, and in many places more desperately inefficient. The danger of her practicalness is its superficiality.

We may say many things to you in this lectureship that may sound commonplace and trite, but we are confident that nothing we shall utter here has greater importance, or a deeper significance, than what we are attempting to present to you to-day in the way of counsel, as it relates to the future administration of your high and holy office. To see year by year a splendid group of strong, earnest, consecrated men emerging from our seminaries, facing with hopeful minds and expectant vision the great possibilities of the profession to which they are committed, and to realize that presently they may be entangled in devices and agencies that are purely mechanical, is an occasion for deep concern.

We must have methods, and we must recognize the value of organization, but see to it that these things do not become your masters, but rather your servants. If you can consistently use them as adjuncts, without permitting them to intrude upon the domain of your spiritual ministry to men, they may serve a good and consistent purpose. Many a fruitful ministry has been embarrassed, if not seriously imperiled, through an excess of indulgence in administrative and mechanical devices.

Says Gandhi, the mystic of India, as he surveys the methods of the modern Church in its approach to his people: "We would have thanked you for bringing His gospel before us had you not mingled it so much with your Western culture, dress and machinery." His demand is for more of the spirit of Christ and less of mechanisms. Must we not believe that in this, he expresses the mind of Orient and Occident alike?

If the institutional agencies of the Church are to continue to be factors in our present age, they must be largely committed to high-minded Christian men and women, who will assume their administration and care.

While we are speaking of the perils of an excess of administration, it were well that we reminded you that the Church of our time is threatened with an over-indulgence in secular pursuits and enterprises. Methods are being employed that are both questionable and reprehensible. We lower the standards of our ministry when we become the purveyors of entertainments and amusements. All too frequently we have been the witnesses of methods and practices within the sacred precincts of the Church that were suggestive of the playhouse or a vaudeville entertainment. If to gain favor and popularity we have to place our sacred buildings in competition with the stage or the concert hall, if to satisfy the capricious whims and fancies of those who are ever seeking for variety and novelty, we must do that which is bizarre and highly colorful, then we are beginning to mark the last stages of the Church's usefulness.

If any confirmation were needed of the signficance of what we are saying a casual reading of the announcements in the daily press, as they relate to the services and activities of the Churches on Sunday, would prove convincing.

The most utterly trivial and unappealing topics, designed solely to arouse a kind of morbid curiosity, fill our church pages week by week; secular themes, lectureships, a discussion of the latest book or play, all these have their place, and the high and holy theme of religion receives scant consideration.

Apart from all this, note the tendency to introduce into divine worship through extended announcements from pulpit and chancel, a long list of secular entertainments that overspread the days of the week. Shocking, indeed, are these practices that invade the sanctity of a brief hour of worship. We have listened to appeals to attend dances, card parties, minstrel shows and amateur plays, all presented with an urgency and an unction that betrayed the deep feeling and concern of the minister that thereby a depleted exchequer might be restored.

Even in the indispensable appeals for financial support, we submit that the greatest care should be exercised, lest such appeals should dull the sense of a reverent worship. If Churches cannot be maintained without indulgence in these questionable methods, it is a large question whether they have not lost their true mission.

There are some proprieties that the Church is bound to recognize and that may not be dispensed with in the interests of a cheap and changing popularity, or the needs of a depleted treasury. May we quote the words of a distinguished clergyman, recently addressed to his congregation? Unwilling to lessen the dignity of the sanctuary or to cheapen the usages and practices of a reverent and seemly worship, he declared: "I more than wish that I could unfold the beauty, the sanity, the simplicity, the depth of the Soul of our Church. I would save that Soul from the ravages of the irreverent, from the ignorant, from the intolerant, from the blind. Blind leadership means the destruction of the Church. Let us try to be faithful to the highest and the best in the Gospel, in history, in the past and in the present, and let us keep a hopeful, watchful eye on the working of the Spirit of Truth which is pouring in extravagant manner, new truth at our feet."

How can one in prayer and praise recognize the

majesty of God, and then hasten to descend to the consideration of things secular and worldly? If, as Dean Sperry says, "a Church service ought to be first of all a classic," surely we shall not make it such by cheapening its character or lowering its standards. To restore the true dignity of worship, to make of it what Evelyn Underhill says of the Mass, "the drama of the adventure of the soul," means to invest it with such refinement of expression, such beauty of form as shall make it a means of refreshment and inspiration to minister and people alike.

There is a persistent call to restore again the dignity and reverence of the Church; to maintain without regard as to whether it is popular or unpopular the high and holy things of worship; to hold to orderly procedure in spite of an age that would bring its pagan customs to the very altars of God; to defend at any cost the sacredness of its offices, and to refuse the Church's benediction to those who regard the marital relation as a form of legalized adultery.

To lift the sacred office of the ministry from those low levels to which it frequently descends for cheap applause and to restore its high claims as prophet and priest of the Most High, these are our solemn duty and privilege. Unless we, the chosen leaders, dare to restore the dignity of this ancient office, we shall find one day that it has lost not only its prestige, but its place of influence and power.

We need not submit extended citations of what we have in mind; we might fill pages of this lectureship with instances of practices, so wholly out of consonance with all that the ministry stands for, as would arouse the righteous anger of even the most callous and indifferent. The lending of this office to that which is common and vulgar, whether to satisfy the rich or win the favor of the less fortunate, impairs its influence, and ultimately brings it into disfavor and disrepute. We may not all have the same outlook upon life, nor need we all employ the same methods, but none of us may do that which injures a cause for which we share a common responsibility. If my neighbor maintains in his Church that which makes for decency and reverence, and I maintain in mine that which savors of the place of secular entertainment, the time will come when the influence of both houses will be seriously impaired.

The Church of every age has shown its greatest power and usefulness where it has maintained its dignity, and stood for the high things of soul culture. Robertson, Maurice and Liddon, Brooks, Beecher and Storrs gave an interpretation of the ministry that we may not readily forget. They scrupulously avoided eccentricities and that which was novel, however appealing and popular, and reserved themselves exclusively for the higher service of their exalted office. A safe admonition to give the young men entering the ministry to-day would be, beware of the alluring appeal of mechanical and fanciful devices.

A further peril that affects the Church's usefulness is the tendency to over-indulge in the discussion of economic and political questions. We cannot conceive that the pulpit is designed for the discussion of these things, nor can we believe that the average minister has sufficient technical knowledge to be able to debate such difficult and complicated questions. Wisely did our fathers separate the things of the Church from the concerns of the State.

This does not imply that the Church has no responsibility in maintaining those fundamental principles that have to do with the moral and spiritual well-being of the people and nation. This solemn responsibility we neither abdicate nor decline to assume. We conceive it to be our duty, as occasion requires, to speak and act in no uncertain way where great moral issues are involved. We have a background of authority in these matters that we may not disesteem or neglect, except to our hurt and confusion. Perhaps in this respect the Church at large has been strangely silent and indifferent. Rare judgment and discrimination are demanded to-day to know the sane and Christian course in discussing issues that involve the weal or woe of the nation as a whole.

On the other hand, nothing is more to be deplored than the tendency to convert the Christian pulpit into a rostrum for the discussion of political themes, a discussion that tends to confusion and division. It is our privilege to stand firmly and courageously for great fundamental principles that underlie and ultimately determine all policies. Men and women will follow the leadership of a man who, like his divine Master, refuses to become entangled in controversies and contentions that belong to the forum and halls of legislation. The fact that we refuse to bring political and economic questions into our pulpit does not imply that we renounce our solemn duties as citizens of the State, nor that we are colorless or without conviction where large moral issues are involved. We will "render unto Caesar the things which are Caesar's, and unto God the things that are God's." We hold no brief for any party, we are ambassadors for Christ and we stand before men with supreme power when we make evident to them that we have our credentials from Him.

We are witnessing a tendency on the part of the ministry to intrude upon every question that has to do with economic, social and political problems. With only a limited knowledge of the issues involved, dogmatic and sometimes heated utterances have been given, that only serve to widen the breach between reverent and thoughtful men and women, and the Church as an institution. It is the function of the Christian pulpit to deal with *principles* rather than *policies*. We do not believe that the pulpit has lost its persuasive power, nor will it, as long as men of high ideals and balanced judgment dare to declare His message and interpret His will. We readily and gladly recognize what has been commonly called the "social implications of the gospel."

We profoundly believe that the ministry of Jesus has to do with life in the large. Notwithstanding this fact, it is interesting in the study of the life of our Lord to note how scrupulously He refused to become entangled in the discussion of questions that were purely political or economic. To one who came to Him pressing his claim with reference to the division of an estate that involved himself and his brother, He declared emphatically that He would have no part in the matter. The question at issue did not come within the purview of His ministry.

In what we have said of a too discursive ministry, we do not in any sense mean to imply that timidity should characterize its course where wrongs are to be righted or great moral principles are to be maintained. Anything like cowardice, or fear of offending those who may be unwilling to hear the truth, cannot and must not be countenanced by him who bears his Lord's commission. We will dare to stand fearlessly for what we believe to be right; we will be ready at all times to rebuke evil, no matter in what guise it may appear; we will stand guardian to those who are unprotected, but we will seek to do it with intelligent zeal. Dean Robbins well asks and answers the question in his *Cathedral Sermons*:

> In the impending social reconstruction, what is the proper place for the Church of Christ? Where but in the vanguard? Brush aside Christ's social gospel, brush aside His hope, His will, His living, conquering purpose for a Kingdom of God on earth, embracing all human life and every human interest and every human relationship in its magnificent loving sweep and compass, brush that aside and you brush aside with it all our social hopes.

The Dean himself is a fine example of the preacher, whose poise and consistency of utterance render him immune to inaccuracy of statement and that which is sensational. There is a vast difference between such utterances and those that frequently proceed from the pulpit. Certain recent pronouncements that bear upon industrial and economic questions have not gained for the Church either the respect or the confidence of thoughtful people. There is a marked difference between an expression of courage that is strengthened and sustained by an accurate knowledge of conditions, and that other form of courage that is a vaunting display of unassimilated and undigested rumors or opinions that lack both authority and accuracy.

That Jesus came to make this a better world in which to live is writ large upon every page of the Evangel. True, He talked of a happy future, true, He beckoned men on to a better and everlasting life, but ever and again He sought to emphasize man's equitable and just relation to his fellows. His two great commandments dealt with the Fatherhood of God and the brotherhood of man. May it not be that we have been more concerned about emphasizing the first, while we have forgotten to urge with like vigor the real meaning of the second? A disordered and chaotic world bears eloquent testimony to our failure in this respect, and a challenging and patient Christ still waits for that recognition of universal peace for which He labored and ultimately gave His life.

That we have abundant authority in Christ's teachings for what we call "social service," which is nothing more nor less than the application of His mighty truths to present world needs and conditions, is clearly evident. The awakening of the Church in this respect is one of the most hopeful and salutary evidences of its present-day effectiveness.

That the Christian Church should assume its full share of responsibility for lifting burdens too heavy to be borne, that it should bring all its machinery as well as its voice to bear upon those ills that destroy human happiness, blight the lives of little children, shadow with a curse domestic life, and breed iniquity and inequity as between capital and labor, is its clear obligation and solemn duty. To stand silent and apart from those things that are immediately related to the welfare and happiness of men and women, is to violate our solemn commission as exemplars of the Man of Nazareth, and to forfeit the favor of those whom we seek to serve.

Too frequently we have seemed to think of social service as a new expression of religious activity that has to do largely, if not entirely, with the problems of labor and capital. The conspicuous inequities, and sometimes iniquities, witnessed in the social or industrial order have very properly challenged the sympathy and interest of the Church. Had the Christian Church been more intelligently zealous at times in boldly rebuking vice and supporting reasonable reforms, had it been more fearless in maintaining the cause of those who were oppressed, it would not have lost both the sympathy and the respect of vast multitudes who, while they revered its Christ, largely ignored His Church.

To stand with fine conviction and intelligent zeal for human rights, is not only the Church's privilege, it is its definite and prescribed obligation. Having said this, let us further affirm, that social service is by no means a restricted and delimited activity of the Church. Very frequently an imperfect understanding of what social service implies, has rendered our efforts ineffectual and our zeal unintelligible to those for whom we labored. In the language of Holy Writ, we had "a zeal of God, but not according to knowledge."

While it is beyond our province to determine and fix wage scales, it is properly within our province to preach honesty and the doctrine of the "square deal," both of which have to do with wage scales and everything else that concerns the health and happiness of men and women. There is a form or method of social-service activity that in its operations discloses not only ignorance but a spirit of intolerance that hinders rather than helps. To be "zealously affected always in a good cause," is a fine thing, to be intelligently informed is still better. There are some very amateurish things being done to-day, under the guise of social service, that are not contributing to the Church's influence or power. To commend an intelligent and informed approach to this very important subject, is quite as important as to arouse the sympathy and zeal of the Church concerning it.

There are some very big questions before the world to-day, to the solution of which the Christian Church may make a large and effective contribution.

Our whole social-service program is lacking in comprehensiveness, it is in the main too academic, it makes little or no appeal to the imagination, it gathers to its standard but comparatively few people. While we give our time to the discussion of methods of procedure, the big issues go unsupported and unenforced. We are marking time; like the halting pilgrims of old we have compassed our little mountain long enough. "Speak unto the children of Israel, that they go forward."

Let the Christian Church feel the call to a great service, let it become consumed, as with a passion, for the recognition of law and justice and universal peace, let it flame forth with intelligent and well-directed zeal in the interests of world-brotherhood, and it will glorify its divine Master and set forward that day when His sovereignty shall be gladly acknowledged by the children of men.

All that we are attempting to say here is simply this, our ministry in the sanctuary and in the pulpit should not, and must not, be embarrassed, or its influence in any wise curtailed by an undue indulgence in those things that belong to the rostrum and to halls of legis-tion.

The wise words of William Green, President of the American Federation of Labor, have a peculiar application, as well as an important bearing upon all that we have said. In a recent utterance he says, "It is not expected that the Church would take a position on the question of the open shop or the closed shop, or on technical trade matters which occasionally cause controversy between employers and employees. All who are connected with industry must be taught that the Church prescribes a formula which has Divine sanction, for the solution of all problems and controversies between employers and employees."

In what we have said concerning perils that threaten the ministry and its larger usefulness, we have not sought to place undue restraint and limitations upon it. We believe in and seek to follow broad and statesmanlike principles. We advocate a service that is generous and comprehensive, as generous and comprehensive as the warrants of our office permit.

On the other hand, we venture to affirm that a too-discursive ministry, a ministry that seeks to cover too wide a field, tends to disillusionment and disappointment, and ultimately to the defeat of its high ends and purposes. The spiritual stimulus needed by our age affords us abundant opportunity for the exercise of our largest gifts. The hunger of men for a gospel that bears upon life's most immediate and vital interests and concerns is our greatest incentive to a service, unembarrassed and unhindered by over-indulgence in matters, that lie outside its well-defined responsibilities and obligations.

Surely the task that is ours is sufficient for the highest ambitions of any man. Surely the evidences that lie about us bear eloquent testimony to the value and importance of that which the Church alone has the power to give. It is to such a high and holy ministry we call you to-day; a ministry free and unencumbered, a glowing and glorious ministry, crowned and enriched with the favor of God, and gladly and gratefully acknowledged by the children of men. "Be thou for the people to Godward, that thou mayest bring the causes unto God."

CHAPTER VIII

HIS OPPORTUNITY

Coming to the close of such a lectureship as this, one feels as one does at the close of a sermon, the utter incompleteness and inadequacy of it all. There are things, as Tennyson says: that like the restless tides, are

> Too full for sound or foam.

This subject with which you and I have to do is such a vast, such an incomprehensible one, that when we have said all that heart and mind dictate, we realize the utter poverty of language to express our deeper thought. Of one thing we are clearly certain, namely, that being an Ambassador for Christ means to occupy a place of such transcendent worth, to enjoy a service of such glowing privilege, to have an opportunity of such incomparable value, as to make us feel at once very humble and very exalted. Rightly conceived and rightly appraised, there is no place of power and usefulness quite equal to it. To think of it as circumscribed or restricted, an office that has large limitations, is to dishonor it, and to be unworthy of its high distinctions.

In speaking of appropriated opportunity, let us attempt to make clear what we mean. We certainly do not mean that outward reach of the abnormally ambitious man, who registers success in terms of emolument or the praise of his fellows. There is a form of opportunity-seeking that has no place in our profession. It belongs more fitly to the world of self-seeking materialists. Not that the consistent search for a broader service is unworthy, nor the desire to use one's gifts in a more fruitful field, undesirable.

We recall Maltbie Babcock's observation that he wanted to find the market in which to invest the gift that God had invested in him, and where he might get for God the largest return. We cannot measure our opportunities in terms of self-satisfaction or self-acquisition. Opportunity in the Christian ministry means something far nobler and more compensating.

The ambassador of a country seeks not for praise or heightened distinction, he is placed in his appointed field to serve only those large and weighty interests that contribute to the mutual good-will and understanding of nations. Our sphere of influence may be a village or a metropolitan center, its bounds, however, are not geographical. Jesus of Nazareth, according to human judgments, lived a restricted life within the confines of a little Roman province, but notwithstanding this fact, He is the world's most universal figure. Our opportunity is what we choose to make it, let us be certain of that.

Sighing for other worlds to conquer, we may, like Alexander, fail to conquer the little world of ourself. The ancient writer had this in mind when he wrote: "Greater is he that controlleth himself, than he that taketh a city." There are no restricted boundaries for him who, like his divine Master, would give his all for the saving of men. Bunyan in Bedford jail became a world pilgrim, Luther in the Wartburg, the emancipator of a people. Blind Milton wrote of visions of splendor, such as no human eye has ever seen; deaf Beethoven, translated in his mighty scores harmonies of majestic beauty such as no human ear had ever heard. The one who said that a man is no bigger than the place in which he lives, had a false conception of life's possibilities. We fix for ourselves the metes and bounds of our sphere of service and influence.

Opportunity is not simply an advantage laid hold of, a propitious happening that suddenly emerges, an accident, or a piece of good fortune. It is more frequently that which grows out of our own skillful manipulation of a situation. We literally make opportunities; we actually create situations, shape events, and compel new doors to open to our wills. That there is a

> Tide in the affairs of men
> Which taken at the flood
> Leads on to fortune

is true, but is is a tide *taken,* seized, appropriated, and in our office it is like the tides of the restless sea, it comes with repeated frequency.

Every life with which we have to do is one of these recurring tides of opportunity; surely there are enough lives, even in a small community, to satisfy our ambition and to tax our skill. We are "fishers of men," yes, and more patient and persistent than Izaak Walton, and with a far nobler end in view. Oh, the patience and persistence of the Master as He waits and yearns for the redemption of a soul, hence His word: "There is more joy in the presence of God over one sinner that repenteth than over ninety and nine just persons that need no repentance."

There are some mistaken souls that seem to pity themselves, commiserate their condition, because, forsooth, their sphere of service seems so poor and mean when contrasted with occupations more remunerative and more colorful. We can make this office drab and unappealing to the imagination, or we can invest it with all the glow and color that has been poured into it by a long line of heroic, valiant disciples, who through the long centuries have given the world its most compelling and appealing drama.

The truly dramatic element in the history of mankind has been furnished by the seers and prophets of the Christian Church. The most thrilling and stirring incidents in the otherwise prosaic annal of the race have been ushered in by those who laid their all, gladly and willingly upon the altar of service. Weaponless, and unsupported, sometimes bitterly assailed, they have literally wrought victories and lighted fires that by the grace of God shall never be put out. No obstacle, however great, has halted their progress, no suffering, however severe, has stayed their course. Even the torch that kindled fires about their feet has but marked the ushering in of a new day of hope and enfranchisement for their fellows. Lifted upon some lonely cross, they have proclaimed themselves victors in defeat, and given freshened impulse to the Christian cause. These were they "of whom the world was not worthy."

To this new age of ours we dare to say: All that you have and are, acknowledged or unacknowledged, is but the gift that has come to you from those who have lived their faith and defended human rights and human liberty through the long centuries. "Heirs of all the ages," yes, but heirs of those "who counted not their lives dear unto themselves." This affirmation needs to be given fresh emphasis to-day.

An unimaginative age, whose genius it is to forget, must be told, and told yet again and again that life's most precious things are secured to it through the sacrificial service of those who went before. You and I are the successors of these men and women of heroic mold. They have labored and we have entered into their rest. The mighty and searching question for our generation is, Have we the courage, the conviction, the will to carry on? We can only do so as we reckon at its full value the opportunity that is ours.

We have endeavored to make clear the essentials of this office, it is now our duty to stress its supreme advantages. Our primary and indispensable work is that of interpreters and dispensers of the mind of Christ. Everything else is subordinate to this. No matter what our seeming success in other undertakings, we signally fail if we do not discharge this, our first obligation. We cannot too strongly stress this. Here our ministry finds its focus, its raison d'etre. "We are ambassadors for Christ." All else is secondary. The world will appraise the worth of our service by this standard, and by no other. We may engage in many things, be occupied with many cares, but here resides the center and source of our inspiration and power. To know nothing among men, saving Jesus Christ, and Him crucified, this expresses both the reason for, and the purpose of our ministry. Surely it is reason and purpose enough.

In rightly appraising the worth of our opportunities there are certain things we must consider. Surprising as it may seem, we must clearly recognize that progress in any cause is largely determined by what we would call consistent discontent; Charles Kingsley called it, "divine discontent." To be devotees at the shrine of the "God-of-things-as-they-are," spells disappointment and ultimate failure. "Ye have compassed this mountain long enough, turn you northward," was the command of an ancient leader. To be satisfied to live on the outpoured manna for which they did not labor had produced inaction and a dangerous form of satisfaction. There is such a thing as arrested development, which issues in paralysis and death. Growth, the absorption of new ideas, the reckoning with a fresh inflow of spiritual power that furnishes stimulus to mind and imagination means to seize opportunities for expansion, and it is indispensable to a ministry rich and fruitful. A let-well-enough-alone policy is fatal to our office. Our best sermon, no matter how many we have uttered, has never been preached. We leave our pulpit to-day only to enter it with freshened enthusiasm and quickened ardor to-morrow. This must be our hope and expectation.

This is progress through discontent or, as Robertson puts it, "progress through oblivion of the past." St. Paul expresses it in his word: "Forgetting the things that are behind, and straining forth to the things which are before." The *Venite*, "O come let us sing unto the Lord," is more stimulating and refreshing than the *Nunc dimittis*, "Lord, now lettest Thou Thy servant depart in peace." When we have reached the slippered age of contentment, we ought to abandon our pulpits. We have all listened to sermons that seemed musty with age, and altogether reminiscent of other days. To our latest hour we must produce, we must never reach the stage where there is no fresh water to be drawn from the wells of our thinking. That is a fine passage that should ever be in the place where we do our sermonic work: "With joy shall ye draw water out of the wells of salvation." Dr. Osler's theory about creative work being over at forty does not apply to the consecrated man of God. Dr. Cuyler was writing and preaching about the fresh joys of religion when he was in the eighties. No man who is dicontented with what he has done, consistently discontented, ever grows stale and uninteresting. One of the things that we have noted in our missionaries, especially those in difficult and unresponsive fields, is their freshness, their enthusiasm, their unbounded optimism. It's only those of us who occupy the luxurious places who ever experience doubts and misgivings as to the final triumph of the Christ.

I am not speaking about that form of discontent that grows out of a desire for new environing conditions, that is ever seeking some place of occupation that guarantees greater freedom and ease. There is much of this, too much, in the ministry of our time.

The only legitimate kind of discontent we dare to commend is that that is ever seeking to "rise on stepping stones of its dead self to higher things." There can be no new door of opportunity without it. Opportunity, we are told knocks at the door but once; we doubt it; it knocks frequently and loudly at the door of our studies, calling us to a fuller, richer, more complete service. I do not know a successful pastorate that is helpful and fruitful that is not marked by progress through consistent discontent.

Gladstone past sixty, feeling the limitations of his knowledge, freshened his mind by a wider study of Greek, a subject wholly unrelated to his office, and became one of the best Homeric scholars in England. He was discontented with his mental horizons, he would broaden them, and the Greek text furnished the discipline he needed. Citation after citation could be given in demonstration of our thesis. Our situation in the office we carry is quite, if not altogether unique. There is nothing quite like it.

Our theme is essentially Christocentric, and yet how inexhaustible it is! There are sermons that some of us have preached again and again, and yet they never take precisely the same form, nor are they clothed in the same language. Here, let us say parenthetically, it is altogether consistent to repeat sermons, provided always that they have freshness of expression, and above all else, an added zest and richness of feeling. An artist friend of mine has been painting practically little else but snow scenes for many years, and yet each new canvas registers an advance over those that have gone before. He sees new and fantastic shapes, new glories and beauties in the freshly fallen flakes. We discourse of scenes more glowing, warmer, more varied in hues and colors, we dare to paint them over and over again, and always with a new vision of their charm and beauty. Turner saw repeatedly, fresh splendors in the waters of the Grand Canal in Venice, and who shall say which painting was his best of this identical and entrancing scene?

All true progress grows out of that of which we speak. I would not have you restless, I would have you consistently, yes, and persistently, discontented. The age moves forward under the leadership of men and women of this sort. The static periods are those where a deadly satisfaction with things as they are prevails.

The Christian Church above all institutions has experienced such periods, we call them by harsh and opprobrious terms; they were the periods of spiritual inaction, the long nights of deadly sleep, when the lamps on the altar were untrimmed, the oil unreplenished, and the sacrifice unoffered. This cannot be in the present age; life is too swift and colorful, too many influences subversive of all that makes for richness and ripeness of moral and spiritual growth are sleepless and aggressive. This is a live age; truly

> We are living, we are dwelling,
> In a grand and awful time.
> In an age on ages telling,
> To be living is sublime.

Know your opportunities, study them, classify them, immerse yourself in them, wrestle with them, crying with him of the midnight struggle: "I will not let thee go, except thou bless me." Age and the proud stripes that betoken long service have nothing to do with it. Veterans were thrown into action when the flower of great nations had been depleted and destroyed. They were the seasoned men and they gave a good account of themselves. Just now, the Church is demanding that the reserves be brought up and into action. There are opportunities ahead. Let youth and age together conspire for a fresh advance, for "the battlements are the Lord's" and they must be manned. We will not bend the knee to the God-of-things-as-they-are, we will not be satisfied with present achievement.

Another factor in this day of opportunity that needs consideration and cultivation is imagination. Imagination is a large factor in the realm of recognized and appropriated opportunity. Indeed, it is indispensable to it. Imagination furnishes the colorful, the appealing, the compelling element in our ministry. We give it altogether too little consideration.

When David came to the end of his reign he offered prayer for his people. It was not for their prosperity, or their material enrichment he prayed, no, not these but, "Keep this" (the consciousness of God's presence and guidance), "forever in the imagination of the heart of this people." A people without imagination must experience spiritual stagnation. We recall Horace Bushnell's fine sentence in which he said that, at creation, when God had completed His work and had made man, He declared: "We have created man, but there is no avenue of approach to his soul, so He gave him the gift of the imagination that through it he might find access to his deeper, spiritual nature."

This gift of the imagination has to do vitally with our use of opportunity; indeed, there can be no real recognition or use of opportunity without it. Logic has its essential place in our preaching and pastoral work, but imagination more. Imagination furnishes the glowing pigments with which we give rich coloring to our thoughts. It furnishes that which makes our work and utterance fascinating, moving and compelling.

Of Jesus it was said that "without a parable, spake He not unto them." His was a graphic, pictorial ministry. He was a cartoonist, a painter of pictures. The whole world through which He moved was a gallery of appealing objects that He readily used to color and adorn His messages. The persuasiveness of things lovely and beautiful suggests His method. Lilies of the field, birds of the air, grass and trees and flowers and hills, all constituted the sources of His word of power. We think and speak in terms of the books we read, He in terms of life. We employ argument, He touched the imagination by painting pictures that appealed to the finer nature of man.

In no place or sphere of occupation does imagination play a larger part than in the work of the ministry. Every one whom we seek to serve presents a fresh opportunity. Every human being, young or old, is a canvas upon which we may paint in rich and appealing colors the glory of the Christ life. We are artists or we are nothing in this office.

The artist is daring, he is finely emotional, he sees even in dull, gray objects, possibilities of beauty. He discovers in lives that are prosaic and uninteresting qualities and gifts that are susceptible of adornment. Go to your pulpit as an artist goes to his easel; the canvas is new or old, it matters not, on which you paint. You can, if you have imagination enough, make it splendid with color, or you can with dull charcoal make it only a blurred sketch, the poor representation of what you feel is beyond your impoverished imagination to express.

Turner at his easel one day sat painting a landscape when a bystander, observing him, remarked as he sought to discover the object upon which the great artist's vision was fixed: "I cannot for the life of me, see what you see." Quietly Turner replied, as he plied his brush, "Don't you wish you could?"

We are, at our best, artists, our theme is as big as the universe, as deep and as subtle as the soul of man. Let us use richer pigments, let us make our work more colorful, let us employ every legitimate method to make it more real and understandable. Obscurantism has no place in our office. We deal in deep mysteries, let us dare to make them so evident, so appealing, so satisfying, that we shall be able to say with the Apostle: "Behold! I *show* you a mystery."

To be imaginative is one thing, to have imagination is another. The first may lead us into unwholesome and unprofitable ways, the latter brings us to the heights of usefulness and power. Our opportunity calls for imagination, it cannot be recognized and used without it. Disraeli in imagination saw his queen the empress of India, and ultimately placed upon her brow a new diadem. You and I in imagination may see in some poor, battered, broken human life, the possibilities of renewal, of emancipation from the slavery of sin, yes, the possibilities of God-likeness. With our imagination we may at length crown such a life with the diadem of immortality.

There is no opportunity comparable to that which is afforded us of being workers together with Omnipotence, in making men and women more godlike. Said Balzac: "Genius is intensity"; yes, but more than this, it is glorified imagination. The painters, the musicians, the poets, the dreamers of dreams, yes, the statesmen and the economists, the men and the women who have enriched and helped forward the race, all, were gifted with that of which we speak—imagination. "He has no imagination," then he ought not to essay the rôle of preacher and leader, be he never so learned.

What a dull world this would be, if it were governed only by mathematicians, scientists, and precise, unemotional economists. Spend a period of each day in the companionship of some great poet; walk for long periods with Him who knew what was in man, and knowing, ministered to him. Get away betimes, from books, and study the ways of the real artists, the true seers, the men who have penetrated beneath the surface of things. What are seers, but men who have the capacity to see. Our present age is the most bewilderingly colorful one in all history, hence if we would keep step with it, we too must bring to our work more of color, more of beauty.

I am not speaking now in terms that are impractical, I am speaking in terms of seized opportunity. Think of the opportunity presented to us Sunday by Sunday, think of the men and women to whom we minister, and remember what a task it is to brighten their lives and enrich them with the glowing beauty of that divine life that was lived among men.

Some of our services and much of our preaching have little of beauty and nothing of color. One wonders at times at the patience of the people; they wait, and wait in vain, for that which gives freshened impulse and renewed zest to life. Our very church buildings are shorn of all that appeals to the imagination. The misguided soldiers of Cromwell would serve God the better by defacing the exquisite frescoes of ancient cathedrals, they would break down the carved work with axes and hammers, they would strip away everything that through the eye ministers to the deeper, spiritual yearnings in men.

There is something splendid about our Puritan fathers, their fidelity to truth, their unflinching and unfailing allegiance to God; but there was also that in their stern, self-imposed discipline, that is uninviting and unappealing. Reverencing them for their devotion to high principles, we consistently wonder whether their view of life was in consonance with the teaching and practice of Jesus. We need their fine piety, their devotion to God and duty in our life to-day; but can we not have these things, and at the same time clothe them in the rich garments of loveliness? "To give unto them beauty for ashes, the oil of joy for mourning, the garment of praise for the spirit of heaviness," surely this is more suggestive of what we have to do.

I like that phrase of the Psalmist: "the beauty of holiness." This should characterize our every service, our every utterance, our every ministry in home, and church, and workroom. Imagination, yes, imagination, God's great gift to us, His chosen servants, recognized, developed, used, it gives us a power, an influence of unmeasured potentiality; ignored, uncultivated, unemployed, it renders us ineffective, cold, dreary and unprofitable. Cultivate it, pray for it, struggle for it, it is the golden master-key to open many doors, the open-sesame to many human hearts.

Says Dr. Jacks:

> Christianity is the most encouraging, the most joyous, the least repressive and the least forbidding of all the religions of mankind. There is no religion that gives so large a scope for the high spirits of the soul. There are moments when it enters the deepest shadows and may even be said to descend into hell. But the end of it all is a resurrection, and not a funeral, an ascent into the heights, and not a lingering in the depths.

Such a religion challenges the finest things of the imagination, it clothes itself, not in the habiliments of sorrow and despair, but in the radiant garments of joy and light, and the overflowing life. "How beautiful upon the mountain are the feet of them that publish *glad* tidings." This is your great privilege and mine, yes, it is our golden opportunity, to be messengers of glad tidings.

Again, in the recognition and use of opportunity, we too often fail to realize that it frequently discloses itself in the guise of some difficult and seemingly unsolvable problem. A world without problems, without hindrances and difficulties, offers no challenge to the man with a sense of mission. A world of weak and sinning men, challenged the Man on the cross. He saw, as no one else ever had, the possibilities of the redemption and emancipation of the race. He took the way of the cross, the hardest and severest way, to prove the redeeming power of divine love. He sought to reach the soul and the heart of humanity by means that had never been tried before.

He demonstrated to men the possibility of the highest attainment, by resisting and triumphing over the insuperable. The very magnitude of His sacrifice makes real the irresistible and conquering force of His love. He faced without flinching, nay, He sought out, the difficulties and problems that had grown out of human selfishness and sinfulness. "He must needs go up to Jerusalem." Yes, He set His face to the city whose tragic and sinister record gave it the distinction of having destroyed its prophets. He approached it with the assurance that its very baseness afforded the opportunity for the greatest demonstration of His power. Every door seemed closed to Him; there was no hospitality for the Son of God from birth even to death. "He came unto His own, and His own received Him not." Having no shelter, no place to lay His head, He insured to men forever the sanctuary of the home.

Paradoxical as it seems, this lonely Savior, by the very course He pursued, resisted and overcame every dark purpose that lifted its foul head to defeat Him. He is the sovereign of those glowing and triumphant hosts who have washed their robes and made them white in the blood of the Lamb. Here in this sublime life we witness the mastery of problems and difficulties, the defeat of forces that conspire to destroy and crucify all that is best and noblest in human nature.

The cross represents to us the supreme and tragic culmination, the dramatic climax of all that is designed to defeat and destroy our highest and holiest ends and purposes. Arnold Von Winkelreid, the hero of his people, rushing upon the spears of the foemen of his country, gathered them in a sheaf to his bared bosom, that he might make an open way for his fellows. Pierced and bleeding, his seeming folly nerved his countrymen and gave them victory. His opportunity was dearly bought, but like other great heroes, he had learned the sublime lesson from the lips of the Nazarene: "He that loseth his life, shall find it." The prisoner who stood that fateful morning at Pilate's judgment seat had none to defend Him, even the disciples forsook Him and fled, but from that presence He went forth the mightiest conqueror the world has ever known. A lonely cross, from that day down to the latest hour, has been the high and holy symbol of obstacles and problems overcome, of opportunities seized and gloriously achieved.

HIS OPPORTUNITY

Though the cause of evil prosper,
Yet 'tis truth alone is strong;
Though her portion be the scaffold,
And upon the throne be wrong,
Yet that scaffold, sways the future,
And behind the dim unknown,
Standeth God within the shadow
Keeping watch above His own.

The great apostle speaks of "buying up the opportunity, because the days are evil," and in another place he declares that a large door and effectual is opened unto him, but there are many adversaries. Of obstacles and difficulties and adversaries he could say: "None of these things move me." Buffeted and beset by trials and torments from within, and enemies from without, nothing daunted or hindered him. He moved, like His Lord, gloriously forward, because of these things. You and I grow strong through resistance. We grow flabby and ineffective when conditions are too soft and favoring. "Beware when all men shall speak well of thee."

No office of which we have knowledge presents more and sterner problems than the ministry, and properly so. We are dealing with the multitudinous complexities of human nature. Ours is not the composite problem of the crowd, it is the problem which each individual life presents. If the psychologist deals with many and strange complexes, we more. If specialists with microscopic study have to do with single phases of life's problems, it is ours to act as practitioners, covering all phases. Each individual life with which we have to do, represents both a problem and an opportunity, and let us be clear about it, if it does not constitute a problem, it presents nothing of opportunity.

A parish is a complicated mass of difficult, fascinating, compelling problems. Indeed, this is its charm. We would confidently say to any man choosing this profession, "Unless you love, passionately love, the hard problems of life, unless they fascinate you and compel you to their solution, avoid this office." Its opportunities are conditioned by its problems. Our lives grow sensitive and understandingly sympathetic only as we immerse ouselves in the harassing and confusing situations that involve those to whom we minister. The man who has never known defeat, or disappointment, or heart-impairing sorrow, can hardly serve those who have passed through deep waters. It was the comprehensiveness of divine love, love that understood, that made Christ, the great physician, capable of ministering to every need and of serving every condition.

Yes, problems are the doors of opportunity. "Behold, I have set before thee an open door"; this, Christ says to every man, and the only one who can shut it is the man to whom it is opened. The men and women who save situations are the men and women who grow strong through conflict with life's sternest and hardest issues. The tenderness of our nature is never so finely disclosed, as when we enter gateways that open into the hearts of those who have been shadowed by disappointment and failure.

Seek problems, seek that which is difficult, that

which has defeated other men; find in those bruised and broken and maimed lives, that have been discarded and disowned of men, your fullest and richest opportunity. See in your Lord's dealing with castaways, human refuse, an example of what your own ministry may become. The clergyman who has never known the companionship of the unfortunate is incapable of ministering to those more highly favored.

> He who fights and runs away,
> May live to fight another day,

but he will never be strong enough to win a battle. To attack is better than to retreat, for "greater is he that putteth *on* his armor than he that taketh if *off*." The sinews of our moral and spiritual nature are not made strong in days of piping peace. The very fact that, in our persistent search for new and fresh opportunities, we do not reckon with them as related to life's sterner difficulties and problems accounts for much of our lethargic and unproductive service.

Finally, our opportunities differ widely in type and kind from those which other occupations afford, because the ultimate aim and purpose of our ministry has to do with the deepest and most serious issues of life. We are not building for time, but for eternity. To use Mrs. Browning's homely phrase, we are not seeking to move humanity to a cleaner stye. We are builders of the stately mansions of the soul. Immanent and pressing as are the surging and persistent concerns and problems of this world in which we live, you and I are co-workers with God, in the mighty concerns of an everlasting kingdom. Fret as we will, fuss as we may, over the petty details and trifles of our office, in its larger and nobler aspects it has to do with the weightiest of all matters, namely, the enthronement and regnancy of Christ. Everything is subordinate to this.

Our present world is desperately troubled about many things. There are more schools of theology, more varieties of opinion concerning the purposes and aims of the Christian religion, more cults and parties, more confusion and discord, than we have known for generations. Happy indeed is he who can keep his head and live a balanced, well-poised life, in such a hectic period.

Some there are who are fearful, who are disposed to regard with grave doubts and deep apprehensions the life of our time. Are the conditions such that they suggest impending disaster? We believe not. In the light of comparative history, ours may be properly called a "new fullness of time." The very exigencies and emergencies of the hour but serve to give added zest to the service of our ministry.

True, our age is calling for leadership, leadership in every sphere of action. As Walter Rauschenbusch declared, the minister of Christ should be "Swiftest to awaken, bravest to speak, and strongest to rally the moral forces of a community." It is not surprising that the late President Eliot spoke of our profession as the "most adventurous," for so it is, and rightly so. We rejoice in our ambassadorhood. We hold our office as one of supreme privilege, of incomparable opportunity.

We would say to the youth of to-day, who are viewing life with eager anticipation, seeking that sphere of influence that offers the most lasting compensations, "Here is one, that in its broad comprehensiveness, transcends all others." It calls to men of the strongest type, men who will dare all for the daring, heroic Christ. It literally means willingness to serve with Him who, lifted up, envisioned the emancipation of men from the thraldom of sin.

The issues of His kingdom await our decision. Shall we have the courage to answer the divine summons, and having answered it, to give all that we have—body, soul and mind—that His kingdom may come, and his will may be done on earth, even as it is done in heaven?

> Mine cycs have seen the glory of the coming
> of the Lord,
> He is trampling out the vintage where the
> grapes of wrath are stored;
> He hath loosed the fateful lightning of his
> terrible swift sword;
> His truth is marching on.
>
> He has sounded forth his trumpet that shall
> never call retreat;
> He is sifting out the hearts of men before
> His judgment-seat;
> O be swift, my soul, to answer him; be jubi-
> lant, my feet!
> Our God is marching on.

THE AMBASSADOR

In the beauty of the lilies Christ was born,
across the sea,
With a glory in his bosom that transfigures
you and me;
As he died to make men holy, let us die to
make men free!
While God is marching on.